A WILLIAMSON **KIDS CAN!** BOOK

The Kids' Guide to Making
Scrapbooks & Photo Albums!

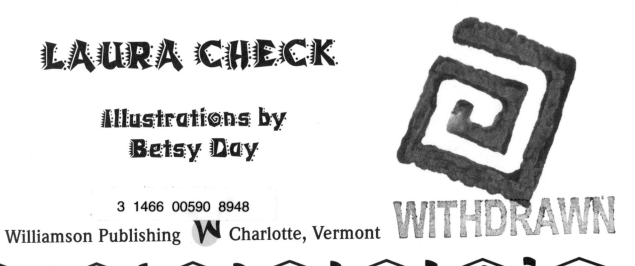

How to Collect, Design, Assemble, Decorate

LAURA CHECK

Illustrations by
Betsy Day

Williamson Publishing **W** Charlotte, Vermont

Library of Congress Cataloging-in-Publication Data

Check, Laura, 1958–
   The kids' guide to making scrapbooks & photo albums : how to collect, design, assemble, decorate / Laura Check.
      p. cm.
   "A Williamson kids can! book."
   Summary: Explains how to collect, design, assemble, and decorate scrapbooks and photograph albums.
   ISBN 1-885593-59-7 (pbk.)
   1. Photograph albums—Juvenile literature. 2. Photographs—Cropping and mounting—Juvenile literature. 3. Scrapbooks—Juvenile literature. [1. Scrapbooks. 2. Photograph albums.] I. Title: Scrapbooks & photo albums. II. Title.

TR465 .C3729 2002
745.593—dc21

2002026771

Kids Can!® series editor: **Susan Williamson**
Project editor: **Emily Stetson**
Interior design: **Nancy-jo Funaro**
Illustrations: **Betsy Day**
Cover design: **Monkey Barrel Design**
Back cover photography: **David A. Seaver**
Printing: **Capital City Press**

Williamson Publishing Co.
P.O. Box 185
Charlotte, VT 05445
(800) 234-8791

Manufactured in the United States of America

10 9 8 7 6 5 4 3 2 1

Little Hands®, Kids Can!®, Tales Alive!®, and Kaleidoscope Kids® are registered trademarks of Williamson Publishing.

Good Times™ and Quick Starts for Kids! ™ are trademarks of Williamson Publishing.

Dedication
To my mother, Grace, for her continued support and love.

Acknowledgments

Special thanks to my dear friend Leisa Hollis from the land down under for sharing her enthusiasm and scrapbook tips with me. To Aimee, Eden, and Isabella, for sharing their SLAM book with me. To my husband, Tom, and children, Christopher, Windy, and Sonny, for helping me get through my second book (which was much harder than the first), and to everyone at Williamson Publishing for being so positive and patient.

Also by Laura Check
Williamson's *Little Hands*®
PAPER PLATE CRAFTS
Creative Art Fun for 3- to 7-Year-Olds

Contents

Way-Cool Collections — Your Way! 5

An Illustrated Guide to Scrapbooking
Supplies, Techniques & Tips 6
  What You Need 7
  Basic Techniques & Tips 10

Collecting & Sorting Your Stuff 20
  Step #1: Gather your stuff 21
  Step #2: Sort, sort, sort! 22
  Step #3: Weed & label 23

Making Almost-Instant Albums 24
  Photo or Art Folder 25
  Easy Loose-Ring Binder 26
  Hole-Punch Design 28
  Make a Buddy Book 30
  Awesome Accordion Album 32
  Wrap-Around Album 34
  Sturdy Post-Bound Design 36
  Simple Spiral 38

Cool Covers 39
  Decoupage a Theme! 40
  Colorful Felt Design 42
  Denim Cover with Bandanna Sash 44
  Padded Fabric Cover 46
  Decorated Canvas Cover 50

Papers Galore! 52
  What's Available? 53
  Make Your Own! 54
    Sponge-Stamped Designs 55
    Splatter-Paint Designs 58
    String-Dipped Designs 59
    Potato (& Other Food) Prints 61
    Nature Prints 63
    Finger Prints 64
    Sole Prints 65
    Marvelous Paper Prints 66
    Tissue-Paper Art 67

Papers Galore! *(continued)*

Finger-Painting Fun	68
Watercolor Wonders	69
Chalk Rubbings	70
Marbleized Paper	71
Handmade Paper	73

Jazzing It Up **76**

On the Cutting Edge	77
Give Your Pages Punch	79
Designs to "Die" For	82
Super Stencils	84
Stamp It Out!	86
Sticker Madness	89

Photography Fun **92**

Cropping & Composition	93
Crop Like a Pro!	94
Compose It!	96
Making the Mount Count	98
Special Effects	100

Creative Lettering & Journaling **103**

Take-a-Look Lettering	104
Pens, Pens & *More* Pens!	106
Extra-Special Lettering	109
Just-Right Journaling	111
Write On!	112

Templates **115**

Index **123**

Way-Cool Collections — Your Way!

I remember putting my first scrapbook together as if it were yesterday. It was a book about horses. My grandfather owned a farm and raised prizewinning Appaloosas. Every summer, my sisters and I would ask him to tell us the name and history of each horse. It was the same story every visit, but my grandfather never grew tired of talking about his horses and showing us his boxes of ribbons and trophies.

One day my sisters and I walked to the corner drugstore with my grandmother to pick out scrapbooks. Mine had a light blue cover. My grandmother got out a stack of old horse magazines, and for hours we cut and pasted the beautiful pictures into our new scrapbooks. We added our own horse drawings, photographs of us on the farm with the Appaloosas, and some of the ribbons. I still have that scrapbook, and I love to look through it and remember those summer visits.

The world of scrapbooks and photo albums has come a long way since I made that first album, though! I've experimented with a bunch of the new scrapbooking products you can buy, plus developed some of my own — like do-it-yourself photo corners, custom pockets for holding extra items, and all sorts of ways to decorate papers with paint, chalk, pens, stamps, and prints.

In these pages, you'll discover cool papers and fancy tools, as well as ways to use whatever you have on hand to add pizzazz to your pages. You'll experiment with lettering and journaling techniques to create the look you want, and find out the best ways to mount and protect your special collections. *You'll find exact measurements, but you can choose just to "wing it" if you prefer.*

Most of all, have fun! Remember, there are no rules for making scrapbooks and photo albums. Design your albums the way YOU want them, and you'll end up with a one-of-a-kind collection. So, welcome to the world of scrapbooks and photo albums — a place where memories and experiences stay alive!

An Illustrated Guide to Scrapbooking
Supplies, Techniques & Tips

Whether you're working on your very first scrapbook or photo album or you're looking for new ideas, this is the place to begin. Here's a quick guide to what you'll need to get started, plus some basic tips and techniques for assembling and displaying all sorts of stuff.

What You Need

You already have the most important tools you need to make a scrapbook or photo album: your imagination and creativity!

Combine that with a few basic supplies — **paper, scissors, a ruler, glue, pens, an album** (store-bought or one of your own design), and **your favorite things** to put inside — and you're ready to get started.

If you visit craft stores, you'll find all sorts of scrapbooking materials and tools that you can use to decorate your pages. You may want to add to your supplies a little at a time as you try the ideas in the pages that follow. No specialty tools and materials on hand? No problem! Make your own printed and decorated papers, fancy cut edges, templates, stickers, stamps, and pockets using items you have around your house. I'll show you how!

Decorative rulers: Rulers with shaped edges

Die cuts: Cutout shapes to glue onto your pages, made from cardboard or fabric (pages 82–83)

Edgers: Decorative cutting scissors (pages 77–78)

Papers: Card stock and decorative papers in all colors and designs (pages 8, 52–75)

Paper trimmers and circle cutters: Sharp-bladed tools for special cutting; use only with adult help

Pens: Fine-point, medium, and brush tips; gel-ink and opaque pens (pages 106–108)

Protective sleeves and containers: Clear plastic sleeves and trays; pockets for photos and collections (pages 16–19)

Punches: Fancy hole punches in different shapes (pages 79–81)

Rubber stamps: Designs and lettering to use with paint or ink (pages 86–88)

Stencils and templates: Guides to cut out shapes and letters (pages 84–85, 104, 115–122)

Stickers: Self-sticking designs and letters (pages 89–91)

The Paper Chase

Card stock, computer paper, decorative papers — what's the diff? And what's best for album pages? Different types of paper have different weights, or thicknesses. What works best depends on what you're using it for. Here are my favorites:

Card stock is a heavy, stiff paper you can use for making the inside pages of your album (the same stuff that's used to make ... cards!). It's stiffer than construction paper, so it holds photos and paper items nice and flat. Card stock usually comes in $8\frac{1}{2}$" x 11" (21 x 27.5 cm) sheets; for extra-easy album assembly, make your covers $\frac{1}{4}$" (5 mm) larger than the precut card stock on all sides. You can buy it in plain white or in colors.

Computer paper is lightweight, and it comes in the usual white as well as an assortment of wonderful colors. It's good for mat frames, message balloons (page 114), and die cuts (pages 82–83).

Decorative papers are sold in single sheets and in books at craft stores. This paper is a bit heavier than computer and gel-ink papers. I use it for all sorts of scrapbooking projects — mat frames, die cuts, borders, and decorative glued designs.

Gel-ink paper is dark — great for writing on with gel-ink (opaque) pens. You can buy it in black or in colors. I use it to make frames and decorations for my pages.

Poster board is slightly heavier than card stock and usually comes in 11" x 14" (27.5 x 35 cm) or 22" x 28" (55 x 70 cm) sheets. It's great for making album covers.

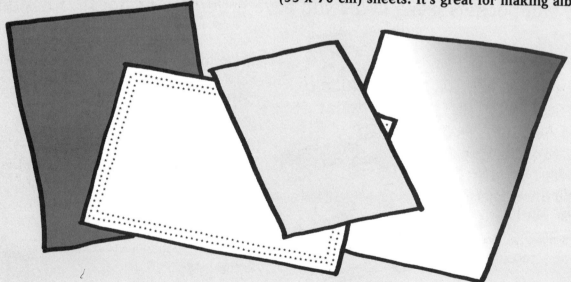

What You Can Collect

cardboard boxes • cards (used) from holidays and special occasions • cereal-box cardboard • clothespins • colored chalk • computer paper • construction paper • cookie cutters • crayons • doilies • erasers • fabric scraps • markers • pencil erasers • pens and colored pencils • pinecones, pine needles, bark, leaves, shells, and other nature items • plastic lids • ribbons • shoes (soles!) and laces • sponges • straws • string and twine • tempera paints • vegetables and fruits (for printing)

Other Supplies

binder rings or old binders • card stock • craft foam • hole punch • paper fasteners • poster board • self-stick reinforcement circles and labels • tracing paper • zip-locking bags

Archival Alert

You're sure to come across the labels "acid free," "PVC free," "lignin free," or "archival safe" if you go shopping for papers, plastics, glues, and decorations for scrapbooks and photo albums. What do these terms mean? There are no chemicals or materials used in making these products that might harm your photos or collections, causing them to turn brown or age (a problem with many older albums). So, if you're buying scrapbooking materials, it's good to look for those labels. But don't let that stop you from using homemade supplies. Check out the Basic Techniques & Tips (pages 10–19) for ways to show off and preserve your collections safely.

A note of warning: Beware of magnetic albums (the kind with self-stick boards behind clear plastic sheets). Although they're easy to use, these album pages are known for turning brown with age (plus, they lose their stickiness so your stuff falls out). Over time, the acids used in making the adhesive and the *PVC* (polyvinyl chloride) plastic pages break down — and may eventually damage your photos and collections.

Basic Techniques & Tips

These tips and shortcuts (gathered from years of scrapbook fun) can help you get the effects you want from the start.

Cutting Corners

To keep the edges straight and the corners square as you cut card stock, poster board, or other papers, use a ruler or the PHOTO CROPPING template on page 119 to draw lines.

Glue & Other "Stickum" Clues

A quick look at what's out there (so you won't get "stuck" with the wrong one).

Glue sticks. My favorite! Very easy to use, no mess involved, the glue dries quickly, and they come in various sizes. Some brands have a more permanent bond than others. Great for photos and lightweight papers.

Glue pens. Easy to use, no mess involved, dry quickly. The various sizes of tips are ideal for hard-to-reach areas.

Glues. White liquid craft glues (like Elmer's) and *tacky glues* (all-purpose glues with an extra-strong bond) dry clear, but they take a little longer to dry than a glue stick. These work well for heavier items, such as paper pockets, brochures, postcards, and ticket stubs.

Mounting materials. No mess and easy to use. Tapes and squares come as double-sided "stickies," as sticky dots, as squares, and as tape. Just stick them to the back of your photos or papers and then stick the items onto the page. You'll find them with photo or craft supplies. Or, try adhesive spray or mounting adhesive.

STICKY STRING

Spray Adhesive

glue out

Mounting Adhesive

GREAT TAPE

Mounting corners. No mess, easy to use, and they let you lift photos or papers in and out. You can buy mounting corners in colors, clear, or plain black. Some are self-stick; others need to be moistened. Or, make your own (page 99)!

Pop-ups! Easy and fun to use. These little adhesive foam dots make the items on your pages really stand out. Just stick them to the backs of photos or cutout designs to go 3-D. (See page 99 for an example.)

Tricks of the Trade

No blobs allowed! One of the tips to making a great-looking scrapbook is to get the gluing right. That means no bumps or wrinkles! When gluing fabric or paper to another surface, place dots (not big blobs) of glue over the surface that's being covered. Then, even out the dots with your fingers. Place the item you want to add on top of the glued surface, and press out any air bubbles with a Popsicle stick, working from the center out. For an extra-smooth look, use a glue stick or double-sided mounting tape.

Oops! Say you glued something and now you want to change it. How do you get it *unstuck?* Try using a warm metal spatula (just run it under hot water). The warmth from the metal will help the glue give way and you can remove it in one piece with the spatula. Dental floss also works well to evenly remove flat items.

Mounting Options

Three ways to keep your collections special for a long, long, time!

1. Make a mat. A *mat* for scrapbook and photo album items is like a place mat: It provides a colorful backing that shows off your photos and keeps each collection self-contained. Mats also make great surfaces for writing notes (page 112) or for making a border around photos and artwork (page 97). Try a simple single mat, or go for a double (or triple!) look.

To make a single mat:

2. CUT AROUND FOR THE MAT

3. GLUE MATTED ITEM TO ALBUM PAGE

1. GLUE ITEM TO ACID-FREE PAPER

To make a double mat:

Make a single mat, then mark and cut a slightly larger piece of another paper to glue behind the first mat.

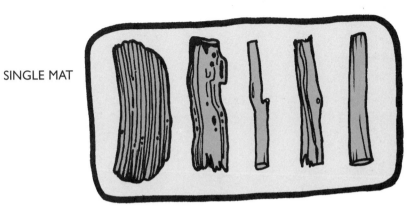

SINGLE MAT

SINGLE MAT

DOUBLE MAT

2. "Window" treatments.

Laminating (sealing items in plastic) is a great way to fully enclose pressed flowers, newspaper clippings, pictures, cards, tags, and other flat items. Laminating is permanent; once an item has been sealed, it can't be removed from the plastic. I like to use the instant self-sealing sheets, and glue my laminated displays onto a mat or place them in a pocket or envelope inside my albums.

PAPER MAT

LAMINATED ITEMS

POCKET

As you make your scrapbooks and photo albums, use good crafting sense.

• Ask for permission and adult help before cutting with sharp scissors or paper cutters.

• Work on thick layers of old newspaper, and wear old shirts or smocks when painting or printing.

• Store your tools and supplies where they will be safe and out of the way.

• Always keep small objects and sharp tools away from younger siblings and other young children.

3. Easy sleeves and pockets.

No, we're not talking about clothing here. These are just some ways to protect and hold your collections! You can buy all sorts of plastic photo pages, page protectors, pockets, and sleeves to hold your finished pages or items and protect them from dirt and fingerprints. You can even get 3-D trays with snap-and-close lids to store small but bulky items like nuts and pinecones.

Or, you can make pockets and sleeves yourself. *Mylar*, a type of clear polyester film, is a good substitute for PVC (polyvinyl chloride) plastics, and it's easy to make into clear pockets. Or use paper and stickers to make colorful pockets for ticket stubs, photos, and other souvenirs. Even a plain envelope will work.

STICKER COLLECTION
IN A SLEEVE

SMALL PLASTIC
POCKETS

LARGE PLASTIC
POCKET

To make a simple pocket:

Cut a shape out of decorative paper and tape or glue it to the album page on three sides, leaving the top open. For templates, see pages 117–118.

To make a two-sided pocket:

Cut decorative paper into two identical shapes (or fold in half) and glue the sides and bottom together, leaving the top open. Glue the pocket to your album page.

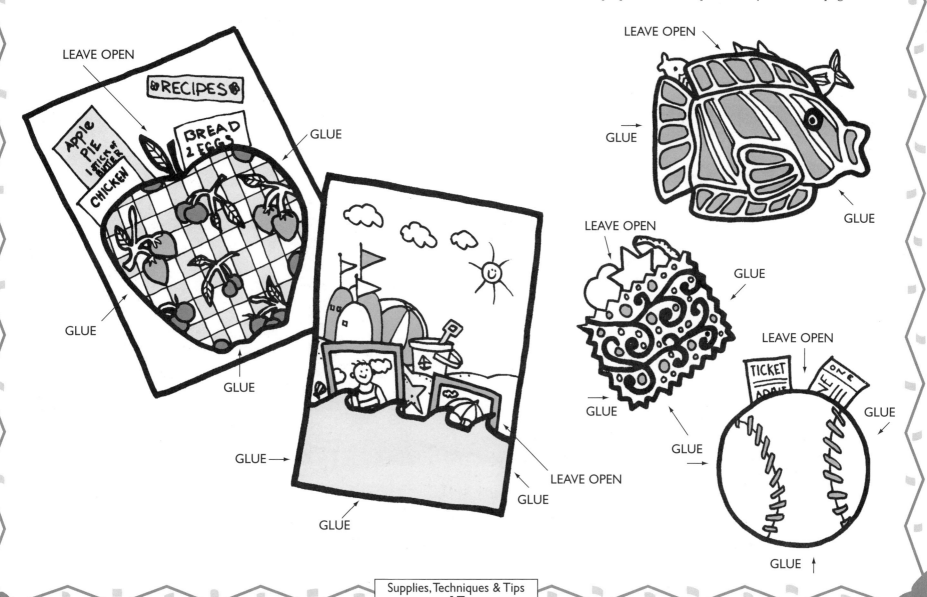

To make a gift envelope:

Trace the template on page 115 onto decorative paper (or waxed paper if you want to see what's inside) and cut and fold it together. Punch holes for a ribbon to tie to close.

Pocket the Extras!

It can be tough to decide just what to put into your albums. There's so much to choose from! Rather than agonizing over what won't fit, be creative. Pick out what will work best to tell the story about the event, and then add a full- or half-page pocket to store the extras in your album.

Collecting & Sorting Your Stuff

Don't quite know where to begin? It's easy. Follow these steps, one, two, three!

Step #1 Gather your stuff.

Your scrapbook can include any item that means something to YOU. There's one word that includes it all: *memorabilia.* It's everything you collect and save to remind you of special occasions and events in your life. Most anything can be included in an album as long as it's smaller than a shoe box. (Even then, you can still include it: Take a picture of it and put the photo in your album!)

Maybe you're one of those kids who has mountains of memorabilia. Your challenge will be to pick and choose! If, on the other hand, your "memory pile" is so scattered about that you don't know *what* you have, this is the time to collect it. Don't worry if your pile is small — it's probably perfect for an "almost instant" album (see pages 24–38 for more).

Things to Include

Collections: Feathers, shells, leaves, twigs, bark, flowers, pinecones, pebbles — even sand from the beach! Or, cards, beads — whatever you want to save.

Family "keepsakes": Old fabrics, buttons or pins, a special letter from a relative, family recipes

Photos: "A picture's worth a thousand words!"

School stuff: ID cards, art projects, reports, class schedules

Scouts and clubs: Sashes with badges and pins, cool info, newspaper clippings

Souvenirs: Maps, postcards, hotel stationery, brochures, ticket stubs, business cards, postage stamps, maybe even foreign coins and currency

Special occasions: Invitations, name tags, wrapping papers, cards, party favors, gift bags

Sporting events: Programs, ticket stubs, autographs, game schedules, certificates

Spread It Out!

Find a good area to work where you can spread out all of your stuff, but where it won't be in the way. A card table in your room or another out-of-the-way place is ideal.

Step #2 Sort, sort, sort!

Now that you've gathered your stuff, are you asking yourself, "How in the world am I going to get all this in one little album?" Well, for starters, it doesn't all have to fit in one album. (After all, your whole life didn't happen all at once, so why should you cram all your memories into one book?) Start small and simple (check out MAKING ALMOST-INSTANT ALBUMS, pages 24–38, for some quick ideas). And sort ... and then sort some more!

Choose a sorting system that makes sense for you.

Sort by YEAR: A *chronological* (year-by-year) method works well for family, friend, or school albums. Sort a year, month by month, or sort each year into smaller subject categories that are meaningful to you, such as holidays, birthdays, sports, and vacations.

Sort by SUBJECT: This is a good choice for albums about sports, clubs, pets, religious groups, community groups, Scouts, hiking and camping outings, and vacations. Keep sorting into smaller groupings until you end up with manageable piles.

Jot It Down, Now!

Even though you think you'll never forget, you'll be surprised at how quickly the details and dates of photos and other items fade from your memory. Use a blue photo-marking pencil (available from photography or craft stores) or sticky tabs on the back of photos to record the info, or write the names and dates by the photo number on a separate piece of paper. Don't use a ballpoint pen or permanent marker — the writing may dent or bleed through the image.

Step #3 Weed & label.

Now that you have your stuff organized, take a closer look at what you've got. Do you have lots of duplicate photos, or too many quartz stones? Pull the "weeds" — no, not the weeds in your garden — any blurry, too-dark, or too-light shots or extra items.

Put duplicates or not-so-great items in an envelope marked "Extras." You can even make a portfolio-sized envelope for a custom fit (see template, page 116). Then, store what you want to use in your ABC FILE BOX. That way, you'll have everything you want to include in your album organized and ready to go, but safe until you need it!

Make an ABC File Box

Make it easy to sort through piles of photos and other small papers. You can buy one specifically for photographs, but it's less expensive and more fun to make your own using an old shoe box covered with decorative paper. Add poster-board or construction-paper tabs for each letter or for separate categories. File each photo or paper under the appropriate heading.

Making Almost-Instant Albums

Almost-instant albums are a perfect size for recording a single event or for giving as a gift. Imagine how pleased your grandparents (or a favorite aunt or uncle) would be if you sent them an album of things you collected and did during your visit! Those special memories are what make scrapbooks such treasures.

Don't worry if you don't have a ton of stuff. Just make the size and shape album you want, and stop when you're done. There's no set length — it's up to you!

To get started, here are seven album designs, with variations. Pick and choose ideas you like, and add new ideas of your own. Then insert your one-of a-kind mementos and photographs. The results are sure to be awesome!

Photo or Art Folder

Make a folder into a work of art! These ready-made binders are easy to use and can pack in plenty of pages, too.

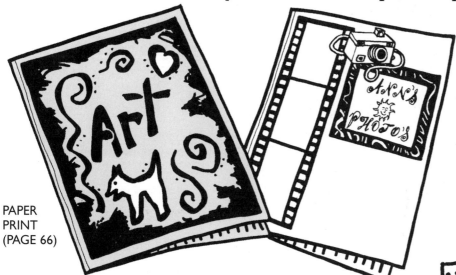

PAPER
PRINT
(PAGE 66)

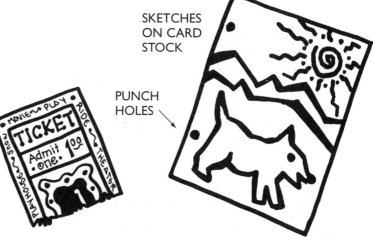

SKETCHES
ON CARD
STOCK

PUNCH
HOLES

Materials

- *General supplies:* pencil, hole punch, glue stick
- *Decorating supplies:* paints, pens, permanent markers, stickers, decorative papers
- Clasp folder
- Card stock
- Artwork or photos

Let's do it!

1. Open the folder and mark the hole placements on the card stock.

2. Punch holes in as many pages as you need. Assemble the album.

3. Decorate the cover and the inside pages.

For more on mounting photos, see pages 98–99.

Easy Loose-Ring Binder

This expandable loose-ring binder is great for small but bulky collections.
Place the items in zip-locking bags, and label each bag with details of what's inside.
Add photos and notes on card-stock pages.

Materials

- *General supplies:* pencil, ruler, scissors, hole punch, glue stick
- *Decorating supplies:* decorative paper, pens, permanent markers, stickers
- Poster board
- Zip-locking bags
- Card stock
- Self-stick labels
- Binder rings

Tricks of the Trade

Snack pack. You can purchase a "project pak" containing rings and bags in craft stores, or just purchase the rings separately and punch holes in snack-size zip-locking bags.

Let's do it!

1. Cut the poster board for the front and back covers about 1/4" (5 mm) taller and wider than the bags. For pages, cut card stock the same size as the bags.

2. Punch holes for the rings 1/2" (1 cm) in from the left-hand edge of the covers, the pages, and the nonzip side of the zip-locking bags. Add self-stick reinforcement circles if desired.

3. Decorate the front cover.

4. Fill the bags with your collections. Label each bag with a self-stick label, using a permanent marker. Assemble the book.

1/2"

COVER

ZIP-LOCKING BAG

CARD STOCK

LABEL

TUNNEL BEACH

REAL OBJECTS IN BAGS

LABEL

THIS IS RALPH

Rings & Binders

Sturdy store-bought O-ring binders open and close to let you add or remove pages or photo sleeves. The binder can hold mounted bulky items, too. Most three-ring binders you can buy hold 8 1/2" x 11" (21 x 27.5 cm) pages, but they also come in smaller and larger sizes.

Hole-Punch Design

Making a scrapbook is as easy as lacing up a shoe or tying a ribbon!

Materials

* *General supplies:* pencil, ruler, scissors, hole punch
* *Decorating supplies:* pens, stickers, permanent markers
* Poster board, 2 colors
* Card stock, 5 to 10 pages
* Self-stick reinforcement circles
* Colored or designed shoelaces or ribbon

Let's do it!

1. Cut two *same-sized* pieces of poster board for the front and back covers.

2. Cut the card stock into pages ¼" (5 mm) smaller than the covers on all sides (so the edges won't show).

3. Cut two poster-board strips (use a different color) for the spine — each 1" (2.5 cm) wide and as long as the cover. Punch holes ½" (1 cm) in from the spine edge, leaving 1" (2.5 cm) between the holes. Cover with reinforcement circles. Use the punched spine as a template to punch holes in the covers and pages.

4. Decorate the pages; then, lace the album together with shoelaces or ribbon (see below).

5. Decorate the cover. Color the reinforcement circles for more pizzazz.

Easy Lacing

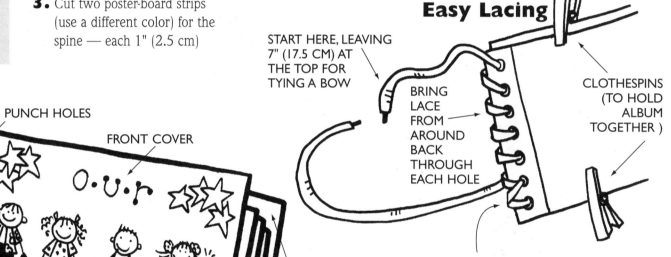

REINFORCEMENT CIRCLES

PUNCH HOLES

FRONT COVER

FRONT SPINE

BACK SPINE

CUT PAGES TO FIT INSIDE COVERS

BACK COVER

START HERE, LEAVING 7" (17.5 CM) AT THE TOP FOR TYING A BOW

BRING LACE FROM AROUND BACK THROUGH EACH HOLE

CLOTHESPINS (TO HOLD ALBUM TOGETHER)

BRING LACE FROM AROUND BACK AND CROSS OVER FIRST LACING

Tricks of the Trade

Designer lace-ups. No colored shoelaces on hand? No problem! Use permanent markers to color and design your own!

Make a Buddy Book

Give an album to a special friend or make a friendship memory book for yourself! Include how you got to know each other and some of the funny things you've done together. Use ribbons for ties, or hold the album together with paper fasteners.

Gift rap.

Include a message, poem, song, or rap around a matted photo on an inside page.

Pocket surprise.

Tuck a little gift into an envelope or pocket.

Lauren is your name, soccer is your game. You have long hair and you really like to share. You'll be my friend until the very end.

Awesome Accordion Album

This simple connected-page album opens just like an accordion, with all the pages joined together. It works well for flat items like pressed flowers, leaves, photos, and artwork. Or, you can make an extra-special card, with photos on one side and a letter on the other.

Materials

- *General supplies:* glue stick, scissors
- *Decorating supplies:* permanent markers, stickers, pens, paints, decorative paper
- Construction paper, 2 to 5 sheets
- Raffia, string, or ribbon

Let's do it!

1. Fold each piece of construction paper in half. Spread glue evenly on the *back side* of the first paper and press against the second paper. Press and smooth out any air bubbles. Continue gluing as many pages as you want.

2. Fold the album together and glue the raffia onto the back (you'll need enough to loop around the sides and tie in front).

3. Cut out decorative paper for the front and back covers; glue in place (the paper on the back cover goes over the raffia), pressing and smoothing out the paper.

4. Decorate the covers and inside pages. (See page 73 for an easy homemade paper look and page 63 for printed leaf designs.)

FRONT COVER

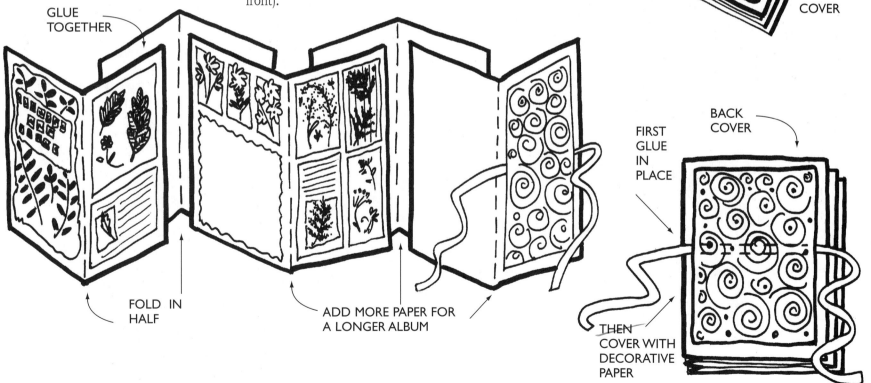

GLUE TOGETHER

FOLD IN HALF

ADD MORE PAPER FOR A LONGER ALBUM

FIRST GLUE IN PLACE

BACK COVER

THEN COVER WITH DECORATIVE PAPER

Wrap-Around Album

Use poster board, decorative papers, and souvenirs to make an almost-instant album for recording school trips or team events, Scout campouts, and family excursions. Along with the photos you took, add details about the fun things you did, and any new experiences or places you visited.

Materials

> ❥ *General supplies:* pencil, ruler, scissors, hole punch, glue stick
> ❥ *Decorating supplies:* colored pens, decorative papers, stickers, stamps, decals
> ❥ Poster board
> ❥ Card stock
> ❥ Paper fasteners

Let's do it!

1. Cut the poster board 8" x 11½" (20 x 28.5 cm) for the back cover and 8" x 10" (20 x 25 cm) for the front cover. Fold the back cover 1½" (3.5 cm) over the front to make the spine. (If you want a vertical book, vary the size of the covers, making sure the back cover overlaps the front by 1½"/3.5 cm on one side.)

2. Cut the card stock pages ¼" (5 mm) smaller than the front cover on all sides.

3. On the front cover, punch holes ½" (1 cm) from the top and sides and about 1½" (3.5 cm) apart. Use those holes as guides to punch holes in the back cover and card stock so all holes match.

4. Decorate the front cover, the folded-over spine, and the inside pages.

5. Assemble the album with paper fasteners.

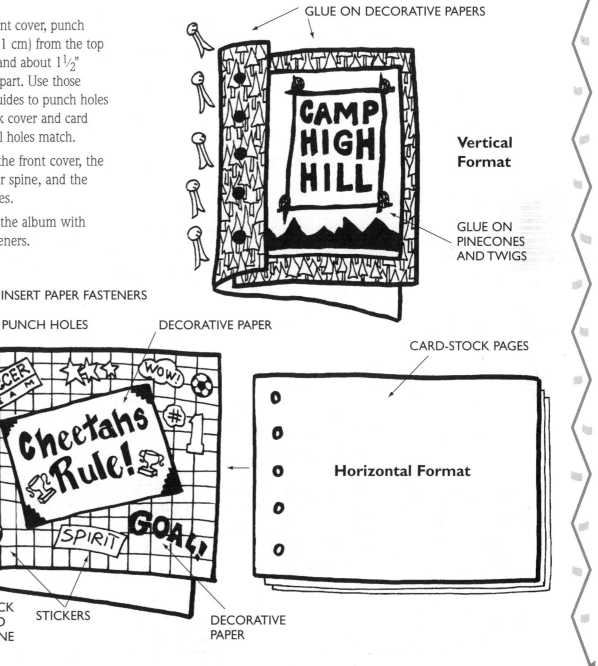

GLUE ON DECORATIVE PAPERS

Vertical Format

GLUE ON PINECONES AND TWIGS

INSERT PAPER FASTENERS

PUNCH HOLES

DECORATIVE PAPER

CARD-STOCK PAGES

Horizontal Format

FOLD BACK COVER TO MAKE SPINE

STICKERS

DECORATIVE PAPER

Sturdy Post-Bound Design

Post-bound albums lie flat, like a book, so they're good for nonbulky items such as photos and papers. The inside posts let you add or remove pages. A common size for store-bought post-bound albums is 12" x 12" (30 x 30 cm), but you can get them smaller or larger, and design the covers however you like (pages 39–51). Even better, make your own post-bound album from scratch, using paper fasteners!

Summer Photos

Materials
- *General supplies:* ruler, scissors, hole punch, glue stick
- Heavy cardboard
- Self-stick shelf paper
- Construction paper
- Card stock
- Paper fasteners

Let's do it!

To make the covers:

1. Cut two pieces of cardboard the same size. (A rectangular 9" x 12"/22.5 x 30 cm cover holds 8½" x 11"/21 x 27.5 cm paper.)

2. Cut two 1" (2.5 cm)-wide strips of cardboard the same length as the *height* of the covers.

3. Before removing the backing from the shelf paper, lay one cover and strip on a sheet of self-stick shelf paper, leaving ¼" (5 mm) between the pieces. Cut around the cardboard pieces, leaving about 3" (7.5 cm) extra on the left-hand side and 1" (2.5 cm) extra on the other sides.

4. Remove the backing from the shelf paper. Lay the cover piece and strip against the sticky side. Smooth out any air bubbles.

5. Fold the top and bottom to the inside; fold in the right side. For the left-hand edge, fold the shelf paper over the cardboard strip so the edge is on the cardboard cover. Press firmly to smooth out any wrinkles.

6. Repeat steps 3 to 5 to make the back cover.

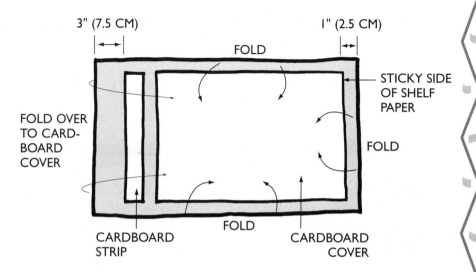

3" (7.5 CM) ⟶ FOLD ⟵ 1" (2.5 CM)

STICKY SIDE OF SHELF PAPER

FOLD OVER TO CARD-BOARD COVER

FOLD

CARDBOARD STRIP

FOLD

CARDBOARD COVER

To finish:

1. Use the construction paper or shelf paper to decorate the inside covers.

2. Punch holes on the inside strips, starting 1½" (3.5 cm) in from the top and bottom with about 3" (7.5 cm) between holes.

3. Cut the card stock to fit; punch holes. Assemble the album with paper fasteners.

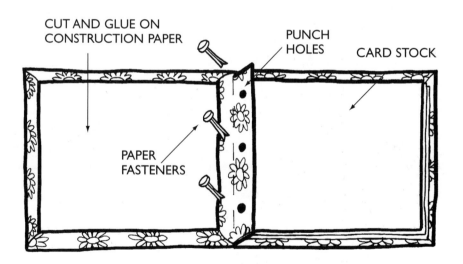

CUT AND GLUE ON CONSTRUCTION PAPER

PUNCH HOLES

CARD STOCK

PAPER FASTENERS

Simple Spiral

Spiral-bound albums come in many sizes and are very affordable, so they're a quick (and cheap!) way to get started. Since spiral albums have a fixed number of pages, you can't add to them, but they're still fun to use and decorate with flat objects, like photographs and artwork. (Our family uses them for recording vacation memories en route.) Decorate the covers with stickers, rubber stamps, die cuts — even craft foam!

CUT CRAFT FOAM TO FIT

GLUE ON FOAM FRAME AND SHAPES

Cool Covers

What's your style — bold and bright, soft pastels, lacy and delicate, or far-out and funky? You can buy albums in all sorts of colors and decorative designs, but to make your album reflect how very special the items inside it are, make your own cover design. Add paper, quilted fabric, felt — even the seat of an old pair of denim jeans! — to turn any album into a masterpiece that's all your own! Pick a design that relates to your theme or choose your favorite colors and materials. Add stamped patterns, decoupage, gel-pen squiggles, and glued or sewn-on shapes.

Can't judge a book by its cover? Yes, you can — when you design that cover yourself!

Decoupage a Theme!

All it takes to transform the cover of any store-bought album is paper, cutout pictures, and glue. *Decoupage* is the art of cutting out pictures, gluing them in an arrangement on a flat surface, and then coating the design with a clear finish to protect it. You can use anything to make your decoupage design: magazine and catalog pictures and lettering, old postcards or greeting cards, gift wrap, stationery, maps and brochures, even photos and original works of art! If you can cut it out and glue it, you can decoupage it!

Materials

- Cutout pictures
- Store-bought album
- Small paintbrush
- Diluted glue (1 part glue to 3 parts water) in a shallow dish
- Damp paper towel

Let's do it!

1. Arrange the pictures on the album cover until you have a design you like.

2. Working in sections (so that you can remember how you arranged the pictures), remove some of the pictures from the album and place them facedown. Choose your largest picture from that section. Using the paintbrush, lightly coat the back of the picture and the area on the album where you want the picture to go with the diluted glue. Press the picture in place. Press out any air bubbles, gently wiping away excess glue with the paper towel. Now glue smaller pictures around the larger one.

3. Continue the same process, working in another section, until the design is complete. Let dry.

4. Brush the diluted glue mixture evenly over the entire design, covering all the edges and pictures. Let dry.

Tricks of the Trade

Cut on a tilt. While you're cutting, hold your scissors tilted slightly away from the paper. This creates an angled edge that will give your cut pieces a smooth, finished look.

Arrange it right. To get just the design you want, experiment with different arrangements. Overlap some pictures; leave space around others. Play around with letters and words, even your own name! Cut strips of solid or printed paper for a border.

START WITH A LARGE BACK-GROUND PIECE

GLUE ON SMALLER OR OVERLAPPING PIECES

Colorful Felt Design

Felt is the easiest fabric to work with because it has no "right" or "wrong" side (page 45) and the edges don't fray. Plus, felt is easy on your piggy bank — for about $2, you can buy enough to cover a large album! The bright colors are great for geometric designs, or you can trace and cut shapes from cookie cutters or templates. The directions given here are for a standard 10½" x 11½" (26 x 28.5 cm) three-ring binder, but feel free to use the same idea for other binder sizes and styles, too.

Materials

- *General supplies:* ruler or measuring tape, chalk (for marking), fabric scissors, tacky glue
- *Decorating supplies:* buttons, sequins, beads
- *Felt*:* colors of your own choosing, or try:
  - Yellow, ½ yard (45 x 90 cm)
  - Red, 9" x 12" (22.5 x 30 cm)
  - Blue, ⅓ yard (30 x 90 cm)
  - Green or other color scraps, for cover details
- Three-ring binder

*Felt is usually sold in bolts of 36" (90 cm) or 72" (180 cm) widths or in precut pieces.

Tricks of the Trade

Make it stick! Because your albums are going to get a lot of use, it's important that the covers really hold together — and that means a good glue hold. I use tacky glue and place a book over the glued area while it dries.

Let's do it!

To cover the outside of the binder:

1. Place the open binder over the spread-out yellow felt. Mark a line on the felt 1" (2.5 cm) larger than the album on all sides; cut along line.

2. Glue the top and bottom edges in place, pulling the felt snug. Place dots of glue along the edges of the inside of the album. Pull the felt to the inside and press down.

To cover the inside of the binder:

1. Cut two 2" x 12" (5 x 30 cm) strips of the red felt. Glue each one to the inside of the binder next to the rings, tucking one side of each felt piece under the rings. Weight down and let dry.

2. Cut two pieces of blue felt to fit inside each cover, hiding the other edges. Glue in place, weight, and let dry.

3. Glue a felt storage pocket to the inside cover.

To finish: Cut shapes and designs from the remaining felt to decorate the front. Sew or glue on buttons, sequins, and beads.

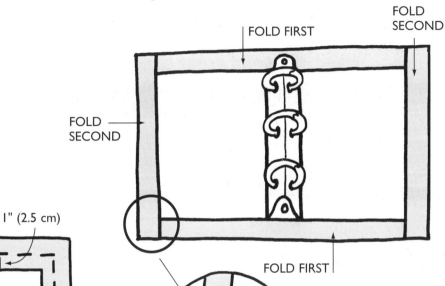

YELLOW FELT

1" (2.5 cm)

BINDER

1" (2.5 cm)

FOLD FIRST

FOLD SECOND

FOLD SECOND

FOLD FIRST

FOLD AND GLUE FLAT

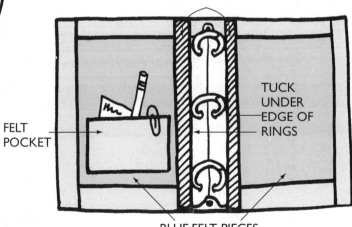

RED FELT STRIPS

FELT POCKET

TUCK UNDER EDGE OF RINGS

BLUE FELT PIECES

Denim Cover
(with a bandanna sash!)

Denim makes a durable cover and the solid color is perfect for decorating. Add stickers, embellish with contrasting fabric pieces, glue on your name with pipe cleaners, or stitch some words in yarn. Then, wrap on a bandanna sash for a finishing touch!

Note: These instructions will work with just about any fabric. Wash and dry the fabric before using to prevent shrinkage.

Materials

- *General supplies:* ruler or measuring tape, chalk (for marking), fabric scissors, tacky glue
- *Decorating supplies:* stickers, pipe cleaners, yarn, fabric scraps
- *Fabric:* prewashed denim, ½ yard* (45 x 112 or 150 cm) or strips from old jeans, 15" (37.5 cm) wide
  - Red felt or contrasting fabric, ⅓ yard (30 x 90 cm)
- Three-ring binder
- Red bandanna

*Denim is usually sold in bolts of 45" (112.5) or 60" (150 cm) widths. If you use felt for the inside covers, the smaller width is fine; if you want to use denim inside, choose the wider fabric.

Let's do it!

You follow the same basic steps that you use to make the COLORFUL FELT DESIGN (pages 42–43), with a few variations.

To cover the outside:

1. Lay the denim fabric *right side down* on a flat surface. Follow step 1, page 43, for cutting the fabric. If you plan on stitching your name on the cover, now's the time (see this page).

2. Follow step 2 , page 43, for gluing the fabric.

To cover the inside: Cut and glue two pieces of red felt to fit inside, covering the denim edges. (If you're using fabric rather than felt, cut the strips $1/2$"/1 cm longer on all sides so you can fold under the cut edges.) Weight album and let dry.

To finish: Decorate the front with fabric scraps, stickers, and other items. Tie on the red bandanna sash.

(see this page)

Gently tape fabric, *right side up,* to the album, pulling slightly for a tight fit. Write your name in chalk on the front. Remove the fabric, and stitch your name in yarn over the chalk marks, using the backstitch as shown below. Keep the yarn fairly loose — tight stitches will make the fabric buckle.

When you've finished embroidering your name and any designs, continue covering the binder as in step 2, page 43.

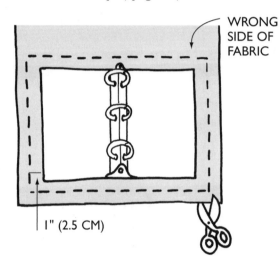

WRONG SIDE OF FABRIC

1" (2.5 CM)

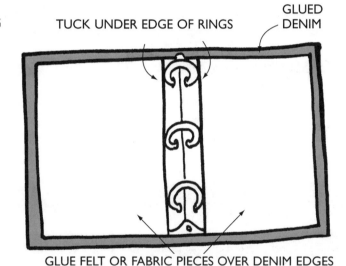

TUCK UNDER EDGE OF RINGS

GLUED DENIM

GLUE FELT OR FABRIC PIECES OVER DENIM EDGES

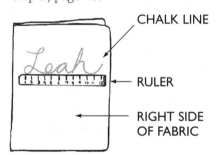

CHALK LINE

RULER

RIGHT SIDE OF FABRIC

Fabric: Right or Wrong?

Unlike felt, which is the same on both sides, most fabrics have a *wrong* and a *right* side. The right side looks like the finished material, the bright, printed side. The wrong side is the faded side of the fabric, like the inside-out side of a shirt or dress. Marking is done on the wrong side of the fabric. And when you glue the fabric to your scrapbook or album, you have to be sure the wrong side of the fabric is against the glue, so that the right side will show!

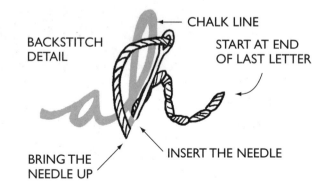

CHALK LINE

START AT END OF LAST LETTER

BACKSTITCH DETAIL

BRING THE NEEDLE UP

INSERT THE NEEDLE

Padded Fabric Cover

Make a padded cover embellished with lace or other trim for an old-fashioned look. For a fancy touch, add a MATCHING PADDED PHOTO FRAME (pages 48–49) on the front!

GLUE LINES

CUT BATTING TO FIT
OUTSIDE OF ALBUM

Materials

- *General supplies:* ruler or measuring tape, chalk (for marking), fabric scissors, tacky glue
- *Fabric:* cotton print, 1 yard (90 cm)
  - Optional felt for inside, 1/3 yard (30 x 90 cm)
- Quilt batting, 1 yard (90 cm)
- Three-ring binder
- Ribbon or lace, 2 yards (180 cm)

GLUE RIBBON OR LACE TO COVERED FABRIC EDGE

COVER EACH SIDE WITH FABRIC OR FELT

Let's do it!

You follow the same basic steps as for the COLORFUL FELT DESIGN (pages 42–43), with a few additional steps.

To cover the outside:

1. Follow step 1, page 43 for cutting the fabric.

2. Cut a piece of batting the *same size* as the open binder. Glue it to the spine and then across the front and back. Weight album and let dry.

3. Follow step 2, page 43, for gluing the fabric.

To cover the inside: Glue ribbon or lace around the inside edges of the album. Cover the inside with fabric or felt, turning under the edges as needed. Weight album and let dry.

To finish: Decorate the front with fabric pieces or a MATCHING PADDED PHOTO FRAME (pages 48–49).

Make a Matching Padded Photo Frame

Materials

- *General supplies:* pencil, ruler, craft scissors, chalk (for marking), fabric scissors, tacky glue
- *Decorating supplies:* sequins, ribbons, lace, or other trim
- Cereal-box cardboard
- Photo
- Cotton balls or batting scraps
- Cotton fabric, 2" (5 cm) larger than the frame base all around

To make the cardboard frame:

1. Trace the photo onto the cardboard. Then remove the photo, and measure and mark two more lines: one *smaller* than your traced line, and another *larger*. Cut along the *outer and inner lines.*

2. Glue cotton balls or batting on one side of the cardboard.

Adding the fabric:

1. Center the cardboard frame onto the *wrong* side (page 45) of the fabric. Trace the inside edge. Snip a hole in the center of the fabric and cut an X to the corners.

2. Glue the cardboard frame, puffy side down, onto the wrong side of the fabric, matching it to the traced line. Fold the four inner fabric triangles to the back of the frame, and glue in place.

Then, fold in and glue down the outer corners and edges. Weight and let dry.

3. Decorate as desired.

To attach the frame to the album: Glue the frame to the album cover, leaving the top unglued so you can slip a photo in or change your artwork.

CARDBOARD

TRACED PHOTO LINE

CUT ALONG THESE LINES

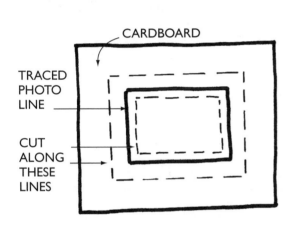

CARDBOARD FRAME

COTTON BALLS OR BATTING

TRACED LINES | (DO NOT CUT)

CUT LINES

WRONG SIDE OF FABRIC

2. FOLD AND GLUE CORNERS

PADDED SIDE DOWN

1. GLUE FABRIC TRIANGLES TO FRAME BACK

3. FOLD EDGES BACK

Decorated Canvas Cover

Let your scrapbook or photo album become a canvas for your next masterpiece! The tight, durable weave of canvas fabric is ideal for a scrapbook cover that you can bring to life with fabric paints, permanent markers, and rubber stamps.

Materials

- *General supplies:* pencil, ruler or measuring tape, fabric scissors, tacky glue, craft scissors
- *Decorating supplies:* pens, markers, stamps and ink, fabric paints
- Post-bound album
- Canvas fabric, 2 yards (180 cm)
- Cereal-box cardboard

Tricks of the Trade

Test first. Test all markers and inks on a scrap of canvas before using, to make sure they won't "bleed" (which could ruin your cover designs). Press the finished design with an iron (ask an adult for permission or help) to help heat-set the colors.

Note: These directions explain how to cover a 12" x 12" (30 x 30 cm) post-bound album, but you can adapt the technique to an album of any size. To cover a three-ring binder, just use canvas fabric instead of denim and felt and follow the directions for the DENIM COVER *(pages 44–45).*

Let's do it!

To cover the outside:

1. Unscrew the inside posts to take the album apart. Lay the front cover on the canvas. Trace the edges. Measure and mark lines as shown. Cut along the outer line.

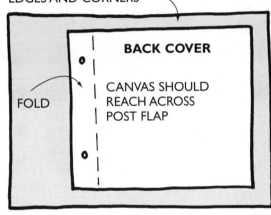

CANVAS

1" (2.5 CM)

POST-BOUND COVER

1" (2.5 CM)

1" (2.5 CM)

3" (7.5 CM)

2. Apply glue to the top, bottom, and *inside* edges. Fold the canvas over the edges. Use scissors to poke holes. Press firmly. Glue the corners flat; weight and let dry.

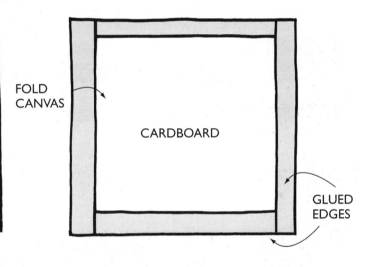

FOLD AND GLUE ALONG EDGES AND CORNERS

BACK COVER

CANVAS SHOULD REACH ACROSS POST FLAP

FOLD

To cover the inside: Cut the cardboard to fit the inside covers. Cut the canvas to fit the cardboard and glue it on. Glue the covered cardboard to the inside covers, hiding the seams. Weight and let dry.

To finish: Repeat steps 1 and 2 for the other cover. Reassemble the album with pages and decorate the blank canvas.

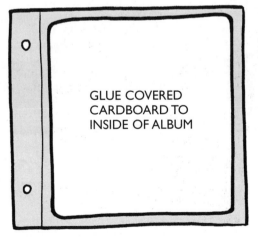

FOLD CANVAS

CARDBOARD

GLUED EDGES

GLUE COVERED CARDBOARD TO INSIDE OF ALBUM

Papers Galore!

To make the inside pages of your album, all you need is paper that's strong enough to hold all the treasures you'll be mounting. But scrapbook fun has gone way beyond the basics. White paper, move over — 'cause there's a whole new batch of colors and decorated papers to choose from. And for a truly one-of-a-kind album, you can make your own page designs, using sponges, paints, yarn — even your fingertips and the soles of your shoes!

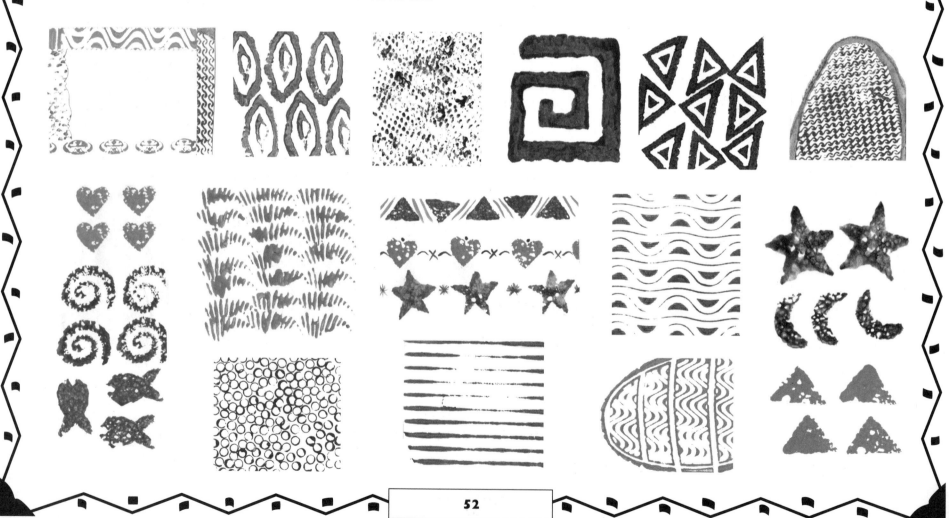

What's Available?

Ready-to-use decorative scrapbook papers come in every color, texture, and pattern imaginable. You can buy pages with star patterns, plaids, flowers, bugs, frogs, beach scenes, and geometric designs. Or, go for a more textured look with raised-surface papers or prints of pebbles, wood, sand, or bark.

And then there's the question of style: Choose a full-page scene, bordered edges, or ready-made photo or mat frames. Even if you plan on designing your own papers, it's fun to see what's available to help get your creative juices flowing.

Acid Check

Any type of paper will work in a scrapbook, but acid-free papers are often preferred for long-lasting albums (see ARCHIVAL ALERT, page 9). To check to see if your papers are acid-free, you can buy a special *pH tester pen* at craft stores. Just draw a small line on your paper (in an unnoticeable spot), and the line will change color to let you know the pH (acid amount).

Make Your Own!

Design the papers yourself to get exactly the look you want.
(It's easier on your piggy bank, too!) Print designs to make your own classic or wild papers, using items you can find in your house and yard. Try your hand (and shoe and finger) at wacky prints; play around with string, paint, and stamps; experiment with marbleized papers; even print with corn on the cob! To get you started, here are the basics for 13 paper-designing ideas — including how to make the paper itself.

Sponge-Stamped Designs

Cut sponges into shapes to create unique textures and designs — or your own checkerboard! Cover your entire page with one design sponged in one, two, or more colors. Cut and combine small shapes for borders and doodles, or large stamps for full-page scenes.

SPONGED TRIANGLES WITH PAINTED STRIPES

SPONGES

CHECKERBOARD DESIGN

FLOWERS ON SPONGED BACKGROUND

Materials

➤ Scissors
➤ Sponge
➤ Tempera paints, in dishes or lids
➤ Card stock

UNDERWATER MOTIF

FUN SHAPES

Let's do it!

1. Cut the sponge into a shape. Wet with water, pressing out any excess.

2. Press the sponge lightly and evenly in the paint, and then print evenly on the paper, being careful not to move the sponge as you make your print.

3. Repeat with more shapes of the same color or different colors (rinsing the sponge out between colors).

GLITTERY SPONGE AND INK STARS

SPONGED HEARTS

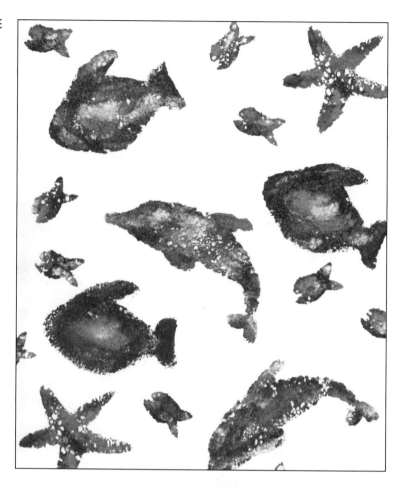

SPIRALS AND STARS

Tricks of the Trade

Easy sponge cutting. Flat craft sponges work best for cutout designs because they're so easy to cut. You can buy them in packages at craft stores. Draw a design with a pencil on the dry sponge, and cut it out. Wet the sponge, and watch your shape grow!

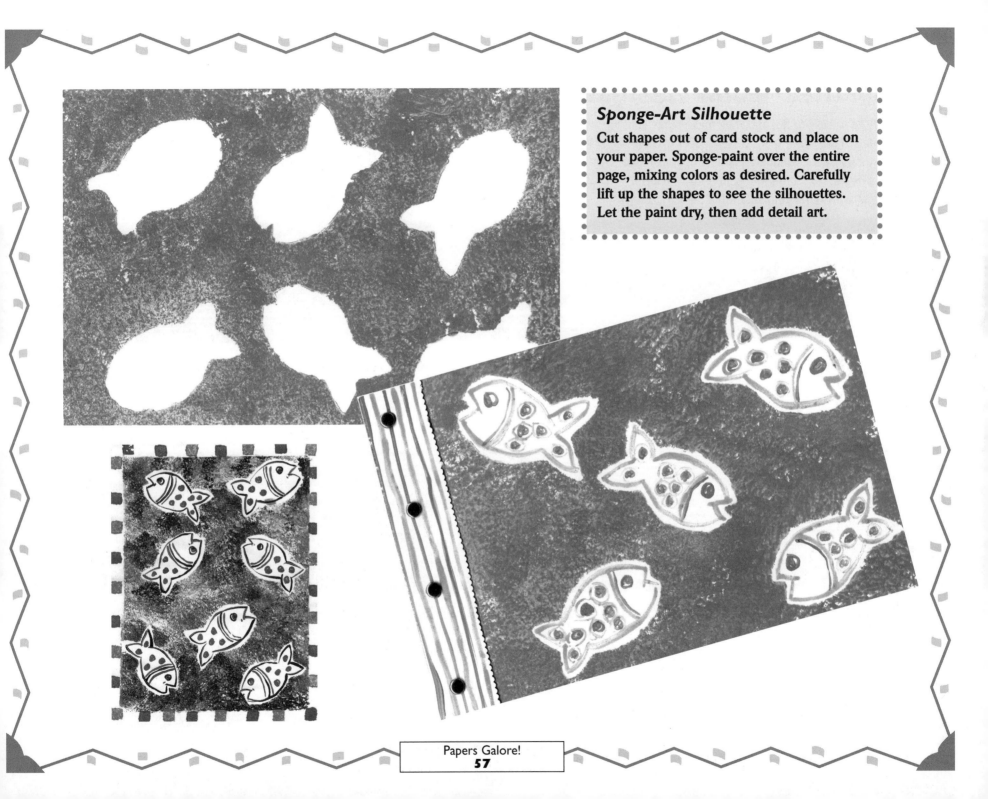

Sponge-Art Silhouette

Cut shapes out of card stock and place on your paper. Sponge-paint over the entire page, mixing colors as desired. Carefully lift up the shapes to see the silhouettes. Let the paint dry, then add detail art.

Splatter-Paint Designs

They're so easy to do, and they make really cool backgrounds and borders! Place the paper on newspaper and dip the bristles of an old toothbrush in tempera paint. Run your finger over the bristles, splattering the paint onto the page. Repeat with other colors. Let dry.

Or, make a splatter-paint negative. Using the splatter-paint technique, follow the SPONGE-ART SILHOUETTE (page 57) instructions, using leaves, coins, paper clips, or other flat items on your paper.

String-Dipped Designs

A great use for old shoelaces, twine, and ribbon! Cut in desired lengths, dip in paint, and trail onto the paper to make a pattern.

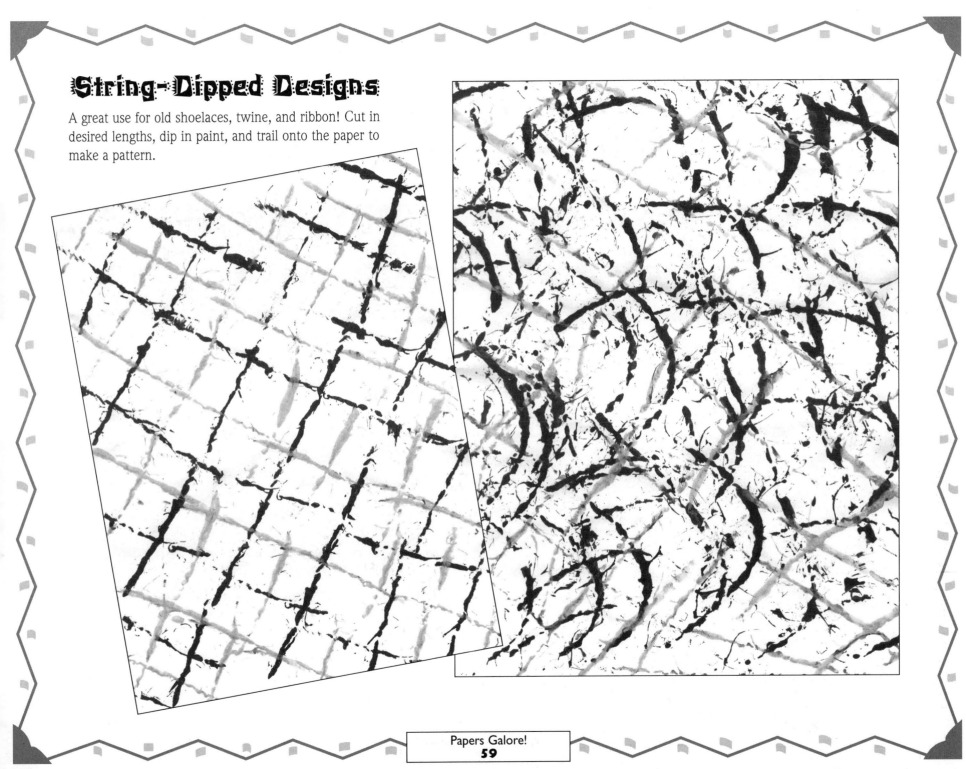

Take a Dip

Look around your house for other dipping ideas. What cool designs can you make with drinking straws, clothespins, and the eraser end of your pencil? Group the designs and colors of small prints to create a pattern.

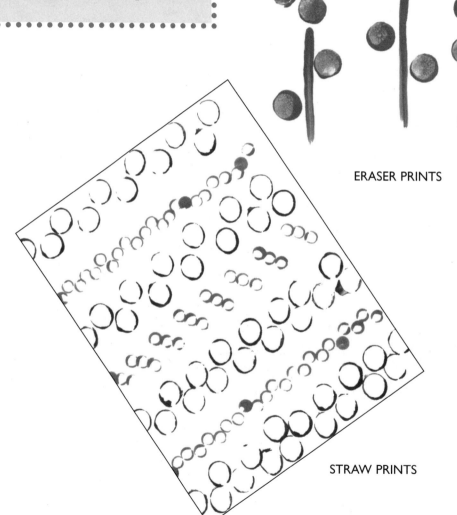

ERASER PRINTS

STRAW PRINTS

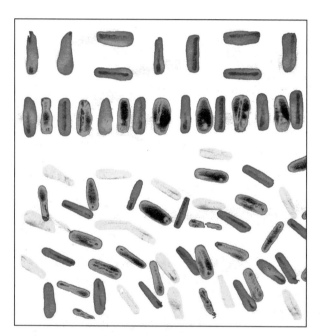

CLOTHESPIN PRINTS

Potato (& Other Food) Prints

Try prints of potatoes, peppers, apples, even broccoli and cabbage. Use for full-page background art, random repeated designs, and borders.

Materials

- Potato (or other vegetable or fruit)
- Sharp knife (for adult use only)
- Paper towels
- Vegetable peeler (with tape over the pointed end)
- Tempera paints, in dishes or lids
- Card stock

Let's do it!

1. Cut the potato in half and wipe dry.

2. Use the taped-over vegetable peeler to carve a design on the flat inner surface.

3. Dip the potato into the paint and print on the paper.

SLICED BROCCOLI OR CAULIFLOWER FLORETS

SLICED CABBAGE

PEPPER, CUT IN HALF HORIZONTALLY

POTATO PRINTS

POTATO PRINTS

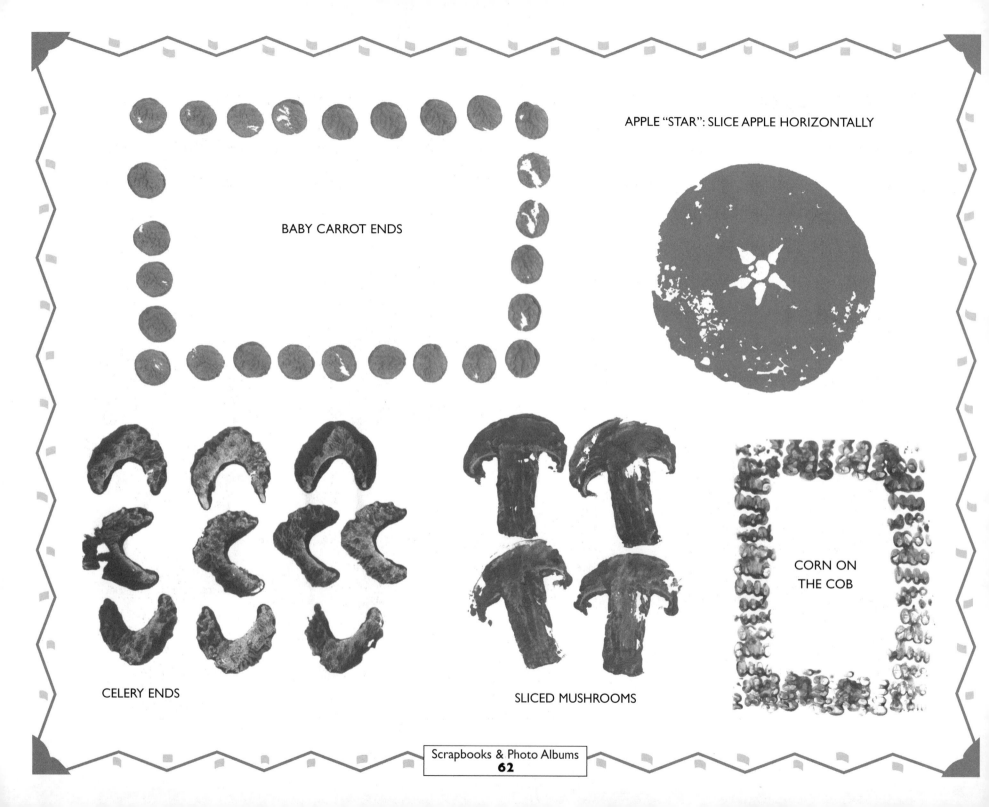

BABY CARROT ENDS

APPLE "STAR": SLICE APPLE HORIZONTALLY

CELERY ENDS

SLICED MUSHROOMS

CORN ON
THE COB

Nature Prints

Use treasures collected from a hike or your own backyard to make unique nature prints. Dip or paint one side of leaves, pinecones, shells, or other nature finds with one or more colors of tempera paint and press the painted side on the paper. Repeat with a new shape or different colors.

PINE NEEDLES

PINECONES

LEAVES

SHELLS

PETALS

Tricks of the Trade

Borders, backgrounds & more.

The size and shape of your print will help you determine how to use it for the best effect. The small patterns from pine needles and pinecones make nice background papers; shells and petals are ideal for border designs; and full-size leaf prints make great colorful backgrounds, mats for photos, and picture frames. Or, combine prints to make an art original!

Finger Prints

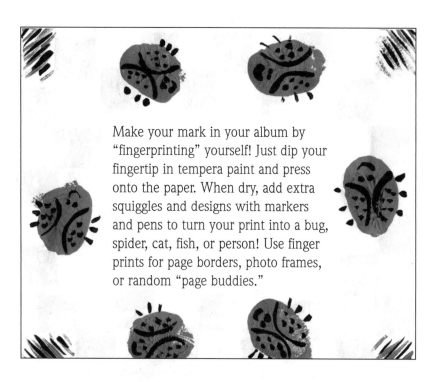

Make your mark in your album by "fingerprinting" yourself! Just dip your fingertip in tempera paint and press onto the paper. When dry, add extra squiggles and designs with markers and pens to turn your print into a bug, spider, cat, fish, or person! Use finger prints for page borders, photo frames, or random "page buddies."

Sole Prints

Take a look at the bottom of your shoes — do you see another great printing idea? You won't believe how many interesting patterns you'll find! These repeating designs are especially good for making page borders, journaling boxes (see pages 111–112), and photo mats. Just don't forget to clean your shoe off once you've finished printing!

Sponge the tempera paint evenly onto the sole of a clean shoe and press firmly onto paper. Lift to reveal the pattern; let dry.

BERRY FLAT TRAIL

June 6th 2001
Hiked 5 miles!
Sunny + Beautiful all Day

Learned to leave trail markings
Ginger roots

Hiked Ten miles Today!

June 2, 2000

Marvelous Paper Prints

Print like the pros!

Materials

- Tempera paint
- Shallow tray
- Popsicle stick or pencil
- Card stock or computer paper, various colors

Let's do it!

1. Spread a *thin* layer of the paint evenly on the tray (a cookie sheet works well).

2. Draw a design in the paint (use the Popsicle stick, the eraser end of the pencil, or your finger), *pressing down through the paint to the bottom of the tray.*

3. Lay a contrasting color of paper over the paint and press lightly.

4. Lift off the paper. Presto! Print again if you want to.

Tissue-Paper Art

Add color (without the mess of paint) by using tissue paper. Tear the paper into the shapes you want and glue them (using a glue stick) for a full-page design or colorful border.

Finger-Painting Fun

Finger paint is terrific for adding bright texture and colors and to your papers. Cover your page with different-colored finger paints

and design frames and borders. Add texture to your designs with clothespins, combs, and other objects.

Homemade Finger Paint

In a small saucepan, mix together equal amounts (say, $\frac{1}{2}$ cup/ 125 ml of each) of cornstarch and water, stirring out any lumps. With an adult helper, cook and stir the mixture over low heat until clear and thick (don't let it stick to the pot). Let cool.

Spoon or pour the mixture into clean jars. Add a different color of liquid tempera paint to each jar, until you have the shades you want. (This recipe makes a thick paint; for a thinner mix, use $\frac{1}{4}$ cup/50 ml cornstarch and $\frac{3}{4}$ cup/175 ml water.)

Watercolor Wonders

Use watercolor pages for full-page layouts, mat frames, or as individual pieces.

Wet card stock or textured watercolor paper with a clean paintbrush dipped in water. Then add different-colored tempera or acrylic paints to the paper. Watch your colors mix and grow into multicolored shapes and designs!

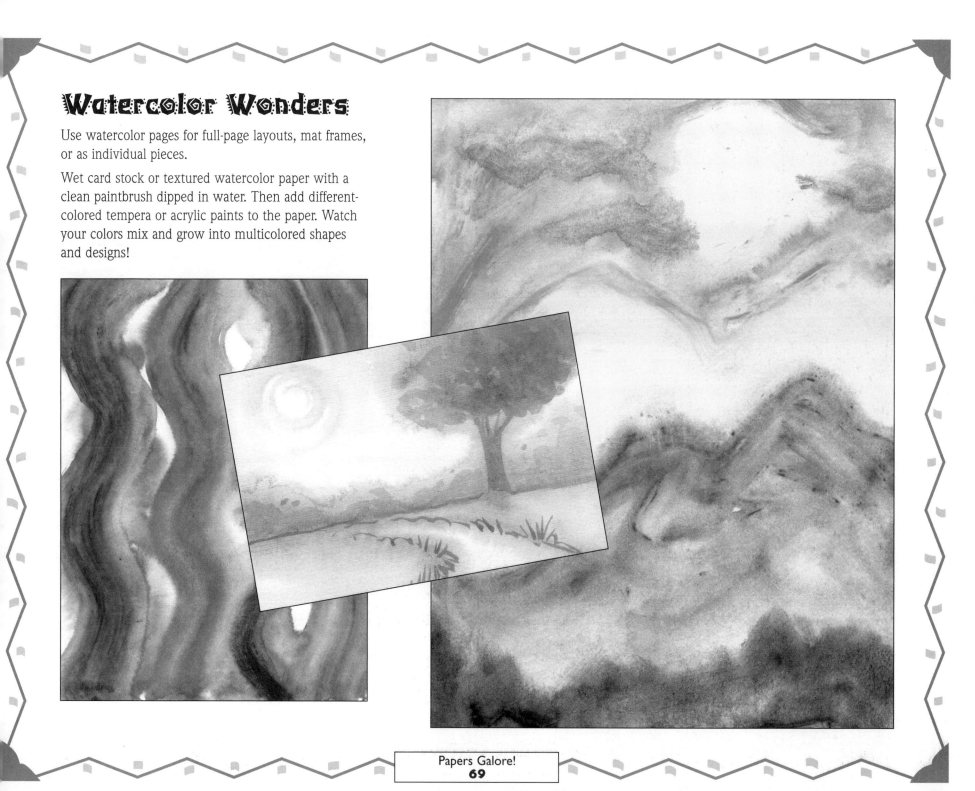

Chalk Rubbings

KEYS AND COINS

Use different colors of chalk for a soft pastel design, or add a textured look by making rubbings. For the best results, use large leaves with prominent veins, wire or screen, corrugated cardboard, sandpaper, and other highly textured items. You can also make a pattern with masking or packaging tape.

Place the paper over the item to be rubbed. Holding the paper in place, rub the chalk on the long side one way (don't rub back and forth). Continue to rub until the area is covered. What design do you see?

LEAF RUBBING

CHECKERBOARD
CHALK PATTERN

TAPE DESIGN USED
TO MAKE PATTERN

WIRE

Tricks of the Trade

Seal the color. To keep the chalk design from smearing, seal with an acrylic spray, following the directions on the can. Use only with adult help!

Marbleized Paper

Looking for a wild or psychedelic design? Try making marbleized paper! Swirl the floating colors and then capture the pattern on paper. Use as a full-page design or cut the marbleized paper into strips or shapes for borders and art.

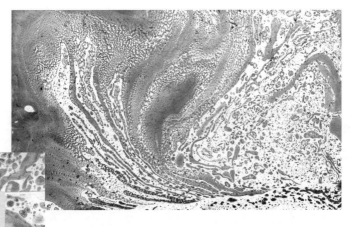

Materials

- Old newspapers (to cover your work surface)
- *For each color:*
  - 1 tablespoon (15 ml) acrylic paint
  - 2 tablespoons (30 ml) water
- Paper cups or small glass jars (baby food jars work well)
- Popsicle sticks (for stirring)
- Shallow pan or cardboard box lined with plastic
- Liquid starch (available from grocery stores)
- Eyedroppers or paintbrush
- White card stock or other heavy paper

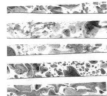
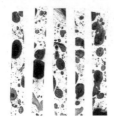
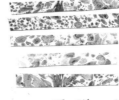
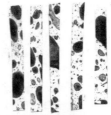
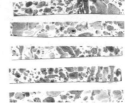
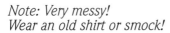

Note: Very messy!
Wear an old shirt or smock!

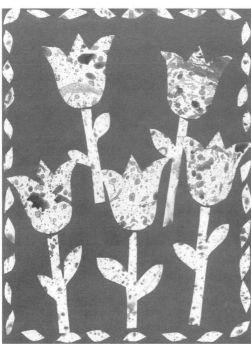

Let's do it!

1. Mix the acrylic paint and water in the jars, one for each color. (The finished paint should be the consistency of thick cream.) Set aside.

2. Fill the pan with liquid starch until it is about 1" (2.5 cm) deep.

3. Add the coloring by drops into the starch. The colors should float. Swirl colors around until you have a design you like.

4. Lay the white paper flat on top of the design. Lift it out immediately, let it drip for a minute, and then lay it flat to dry.

5. Gently stir the surface of the pan or add a new color for the next print.

Tricks of the Trade

Awesome Art

- Don't worry about making any mistakes — each design is unique and interesting! For best results, use two or three colors and swirl, but don't stir the colors in — you want them to remain on the surface.

- Use pencils, pins, or combs to make intricate designs. Swirl paints with a comb; use an eyedropper to drop paints on top of each other for a bull's-eye effect; drag a pencil or pin out from the center of the drop to create a star.

- Dip poster board to make an album cover.

Handmade Paper

Handmade paper gives your album pages and covers a personal touch (and by recycling old paper, you do your part for the environment!). Plus, handmade paper doesn't contain as many chemicals as machine-made paper, so it's great for albums. Make yours from paper scraps, and then press the pulp — and carry on traditions similar to those of thousands of years ago, when the first paper was made from papyrus plants. But please don't pour the leftover pulp down the sink — it will clog the drain!

Materials

- Old newspapers (to cover your work surface)
- Paper scraps (newsprint will give your paper a blue tone)
- Bowl
- Water
- Blender
- Wire mesh or screen (a piece that will fit in the dishpan)
- Dishpan
- Old sheets and towels
- Sponge
- Rolling pin

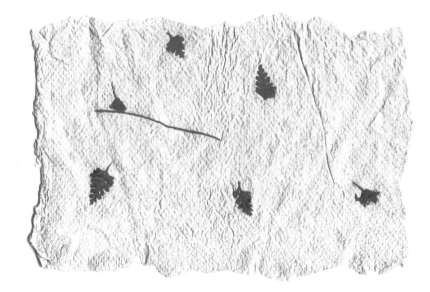

Let's do it!

To make the pulp:

1. Tear scraps into small pieces and soak in warm water for 30 minutes or overnight.

2. Fill the blender half full of water; add a handful of the soaked paper.

3. Blend until you have a soup-like mush (pulp!).

To make the paper:

1. Lay the screen in the dish-pan. Fill with about 3" (7.5 cm) of water. Add the pulp.

2. Slowly slide the screen back and forth through the mixture, and then lift it straight up. You want the pulp evenly distributed on the screen.

3. Set the screen on an old towel to drain. Then lay a piece of old sheet on top of the pulp and press gently with a sponge to remove the excess water.

4. Turn the screen and the sheet over, letting the paper fall onto the sheet. Cover with a dry towel and use a rolling pin to squeeze out more water. (This also strengthens and bonds the paper.)

5. Let the paper dry overnight. To speed up the process, ask an adult to use a hair dryer or to cover the paper with a clean sheet and then iron it. When the paper is dry, carefully peel it from the sheet.

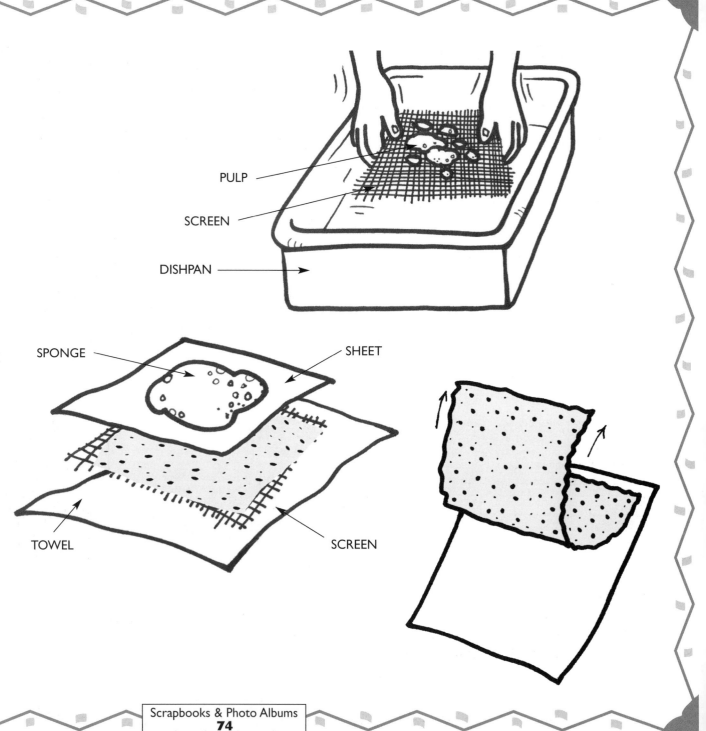

PULP

SCREEN

DISHPAN

SPONGE

SHEET

TOWEL

SCREEN

Make a Mold & Deckle

If you're making lots of paper and want it to be about the same size and shape, you'll need a *mold* (a frame with a screen) and *deckle* (an empty frame). The mold is used screen side up to catch the paper fibers; the deckle is used to shape the paper's edges.

To make a mold and deckle, you'll need two wooden picture frames of the same size (without the glass), wire screen, and tacks or staples. Set aside one frame for the deckle; tack the screen to the other frame.

To use them, hold the deckle firmly against the mold, with the screen side up, and dip it into the pulp in the dishpan. Lift it up when you have an even layer of pulp, and set the frames on a towel to drain. Remove the deckle. Gently place the mold on a clean sheet or towel and continue as in step 3, page 74.

Tricks of the Trade

Pretty Paper

• Add food coloring to the pulp or blend in bits of colored construction paper.

• Press dried flower petals, ferns, weeds, leaves, or grasses into the wet pulp.

• Add sparkles or snippets of ribbon to the paper mixture.

• Scent it! Add vanilla, almond, lemon, or coconut extracts to the dishpan water.

DECKLE

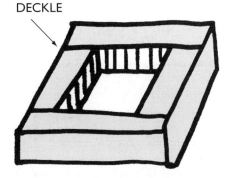

TACK OR STAPLE
SCREEN TO MOLD

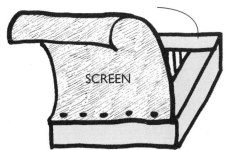

SCREEN

Aged to a Tea

Want paper that looks old? Crumple it, then unfold it and place it flat in a tray or pan. Pour cold tea over it. Let it soak for 15 minutes, then carefully lift it out and hang your "aged" paper to dry.

Jazzing It Up

Edgers, punches, die cuts — say what? Are these some kind of new gardening tools? No, actually, they're just some of the many supplies available for adding details and designs to your scrapbook or photo album pages. Plus, the old familiar favorites —

stickers, rubber stamps, and stencils — now come in oodles of new, hip designs as well. Looking for even more creativity? Make awesome embellishments yourself — using homemade stamps, stencils, die cuts, and more!

Friends are flowers in the Garden of life.

On the Cutting Edge

Have you ever used "pinking shears" for making a fancy edge on fabric? Then you have a good idea of what edgers are. *Edgers* are just fancy-bladed scissors that cut edges or corner designs on paper. You can buy them in lots of styles, with each design having a special name, like Lightning, Cotton Candy, Clouds, or Seagulls.

Edgers take a little practice to use, and some designs are easier to cut than others. For best results:

- Don't cut all the way to the end of the scissors' blade. Stop just before the end; then line up the design and cut again.

- To match corners, start and stop in the corners of a mat frame, using the middle of the edgers' blade design for your first cut. That way, your corner designs will match.

Once you get the hang of it, use edgers to trim your mat frames, make intricate borders, or to cut out cool-looking letters and shapes. Here are some other techniques you can try:

- Flip your edgers over and cut in the opposite direction for a different design.

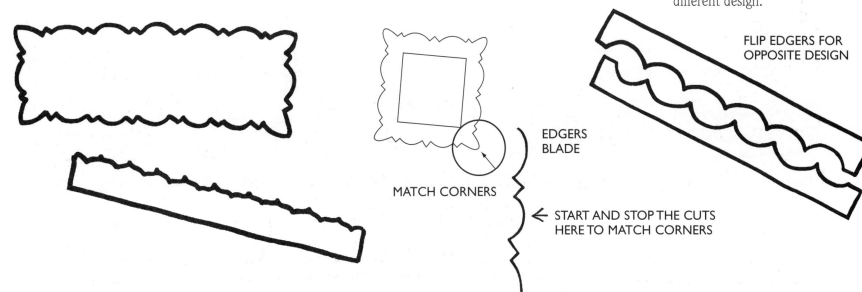

FLIP EDGERS FOR OPPOSITE DESIGN

EDGERS BLADE

MATCH CORNERS

← START AND STOP THE CUTS HERE TO MATCH CORNERS

- Use two different-edged designs on a mat or border. Or double up designs and add some of your own for a unique look!

DOUBLE MAT WITH TWO EDGED DESIGNS

TRIPLE MAT WITH STAMPED BACKGROUND

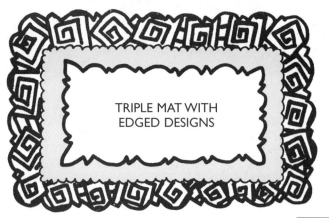

TRIPLE MAT WITH EDGED DESIGNS

Make Your Own Edgers
(for only a few cents!)

Glue pennies in a row on a piece of cardboard. Use a pencil to trace the edge, then cut the design out. You'll have two different-edged designs!

OPPOSITE EDGED DESIGNS

For a jagged edge, tape triangle shapes (trimmed from cardboard corners) to a cardboard guide. Trace and cut out.

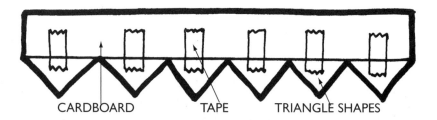

CARDBOARD   TAPE   TRIANGLE SHAPES

Tricks of the Trade

Sharpen those edges! No, we're not talking about skis or ice skates. If the edges of your edgers are grabbing instead of cutting clean, sharpen them by cutting through a piece of aluminum foil or waxed paper several times. (This works for sharpening punches, too — see page 79).

Give Your Pages Punch

Punches are just like a hole punch, except these versions produce fancy designs of all sorts of shapes and sizes. You can buy punches in mini, small, medium, and large sizes, and in practically every shape imaginable: hearts, stars, horses, teddy bears, birthday cakes, bones, bicycles, cars, candy, clouds, baseball players, helicopters, music notes, tropical fish, spirals, squares — you name it! You punch the design out of paper, making a *silhouette*. You can also use the punched-out pieces (called *punch confetti*) to make a different design. (Or, buy these pieces separately.)

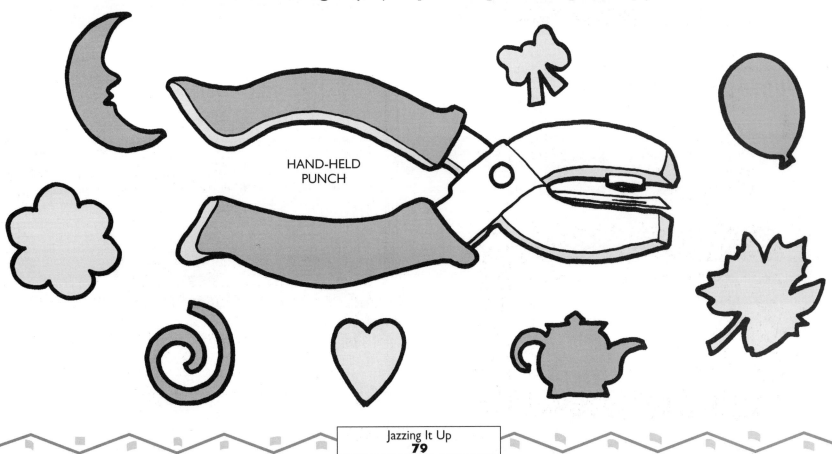

HAND-HELD
PUNCH

Some punches make single shapes; others make more intricate designs, that are great for borders. Or, make your own borders using single punches and a ruler.

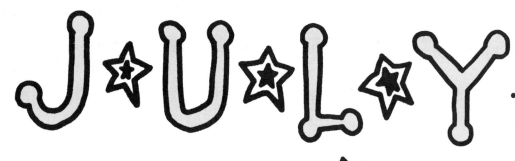

• Use punch confetti to jazz up your words.

• Combine punch confetti into fancy designs or cut them to make new designs.

PUNCHED BORDERS

HEARTS AND CUT STARS

COMBINED DESIGNS

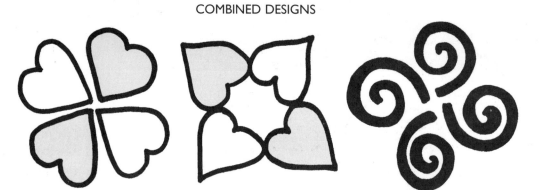

- Use your punched-out scraps to make stencils. (For more on make-your-own stencils, see page 85.)

- Combine with edgers and art!

PUNCHED STENCIL

PUNCH CONFETTI WITH EDGED MATS

PUNCH CONFETTI BORDER WITH ART DETAIL

Tricks of the Trade

Punch guide. To line up your punches evenly, use the side of the punch as your guide for the next punch. Or mark where you want each punch with a pencil and ruler; then, turn your punch upside down so you can see your pencil mark and punch.

Sticky punches? Try punching through aluminum foil, waxed paper, or a light-grade sandpaper a few times. I've found sticking the punch in the freezer for a few minutes really helps, too!

Safe storage. A fishing tackle box works great for storing punches and edgers.

Designs to "Die" For

Die cuts, a fancy name for cutout paper shapes, add flair and fun to your pages, and they're super simple to make. You can cut out your own from almost anything. My favorite source for exciting color combos and designs is old cards. Just take a look and you'll see ready-to-cut-out borders and die-cut designs you can use to frame a photo or create a scene. Also keep your eye out for cool die-cut ideas from gift wrap, coloring books, old picture books, magazines, and advertisements.

DIE CUTS
FROM CARDS

GOOD CARD
FOR CUTOUTS

FRAME
BORDERS
FROM
CARDS

You can also buy precut die cuts, or make your own from paper-doll cutouts, felt-board designs, or stencils.

PAPER DOLL- AND STORE-BOUGHT DIE CUTS

STORE-BOUGHT DIE CUTS

LAKE FLORAS

AUGUST 2000

Super Stencils

Stencils are the reverse of die cuts: They're the cardboard or plastic sheets left over when a design is cut out. You just hold the stencil tight and then fill in the design with markers, pens, or sponge paints to create borders, mat frames, or doodles anywhere you like! Or you can trace and cut out the designs to make your own die cuts. Stencils have come a long way since the days of the alphabet-only designs. Now, in addition to a whole slew of alphabets, you can choose from single designs (like animals and stars), full-page themes (beach party, camping trip, circus fun), fancy ruler edge designs, oval and rectangular photo frame stencils, and all sorts of cool shapes.

And for any stencils you can't find, you can simply make your own!

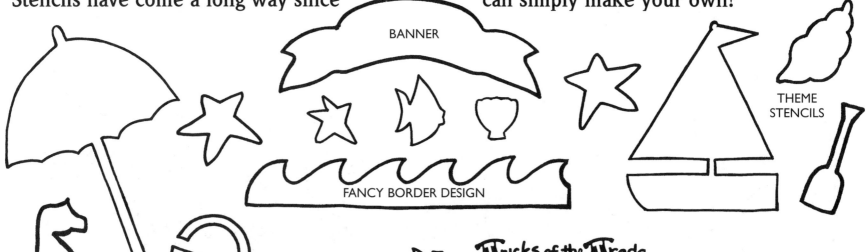

BANNER

THEME STENCILS

FANCY BORDER DESIGN

Tricks of the Trade

Hold tight! When tracing or filling in the design, hold the stencil sheet down firmly so the design won't shift. Use gentle pressure to trace around the design edge slowly (your pencil or pen will want to jump off the edge or slide under the template). Blend in any blips with other doodles and designs.

Do-It-Yourself Stencils

Looking for a stencil? Try the kitchen! Cookie cutters make great stencils. Trace, and then fill in a design or cut out a design or photo frame. Just place the cookie cutter over a photo or paper and lightly trace the outline; then, cut out the shape. Or, to make your own stencil, trace the design onto a plastic lid or a piece of cardboard and then cut out the center.

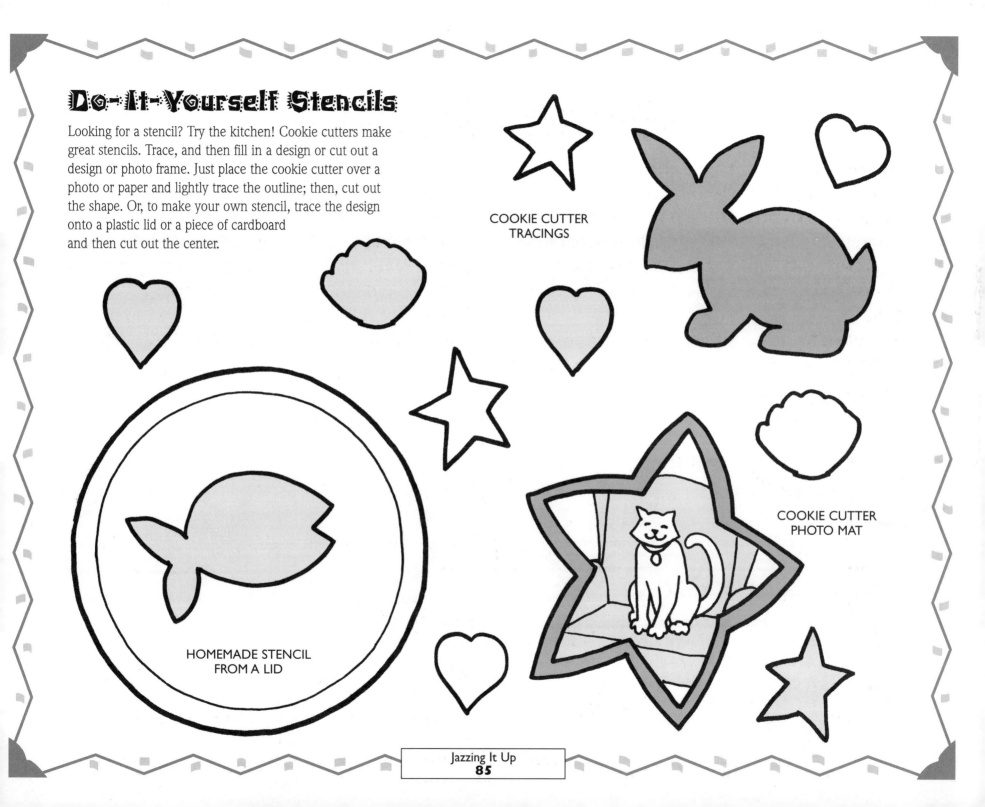

COOKIE CUTTER
TRACINGS

COOKIE CUTTER
PHOTO MAT

HOMEMADE STENCIL
FROM A LID

Stamp It Out!

If you wanted to, you could do your whole album using rubber stamps — and you'd never run out of designs! There are so many to choose from! Stamp sizes range from ½" (1 cm) to 6" (15 cm), with single designs, to alphabet fonts and sayings, to stamps you piece together. Use stamps for whole-page backgrounds, borders, corners, and mat frames; add decorations to lettering and words; or stamp out a complete scene or album cover.

Go for the Color

Give your stamps some personality! Add color to your stamped designs by stamping a dark color for the outline, then fill in with different-colored markers. Or add two or three colors right on the stamp.

MARKER DETAILING

Tricks of the Trade

Practice makes perfect. Before you actually stamp the image on your album page, practice stamping it a few times on a piece of scrap paper so you get the feel of how much pressure to use on the ink pad. Be sure to press straight down and apply even pressure.

Line it up. To place your stamp right where you want it, line up the side of the stamp. Make a mark on the edge, or back of your stamp where the design starts and stops so you know where the next one will be.

Ink ideas. Any kind of ink will work, but it's best to use pigment inks, because they're permanent — they won't run if your page gets wet and they won't fade. Always clean your stamps (a damp paper towel works fine) before you put them away. Then store them facedown.

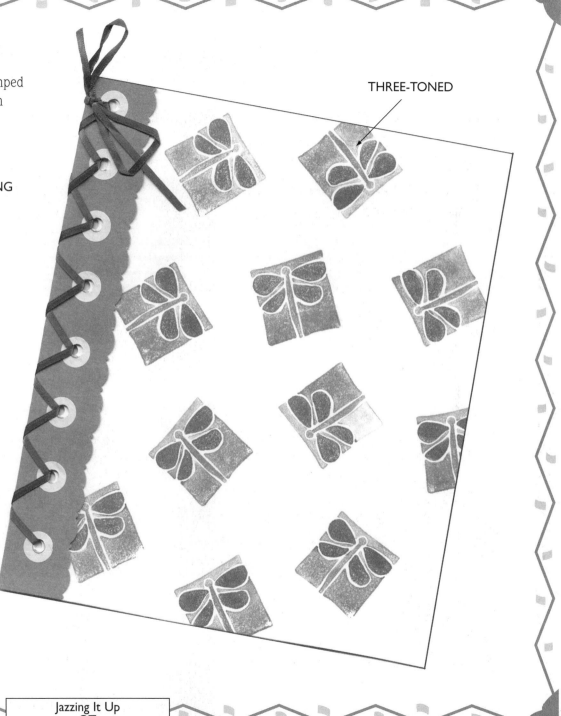

THREE-TONED

Make a Stamp!

To make a soap stamp: Draw a design in a bar of soap with a pen or pencil. (Soap is so soft you can easily make a mark about $1/4"/5$ mm deep.) Using the end of a vegetable peeler or a table knife (not the sharp kind!), carefully cut around the design. Scrape the extra soap away.

To make an eraser stamp: Draw a simple design on the flat side of an eraser. Have an adult help you carve out your design or cut away the excess, using a utility knife.

To make sponge and string stamps: Print with a cut piece of sponge (see SPONGE-STAMPED DESIGNS, page 55).

A strip of cardboard, folded into thirds, makes an ideal base and provides a handle for easy stamping. Or, glue several pieces of sponge into a more intricate design.

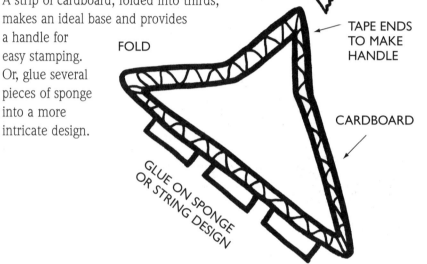

TAPE ENDS TO MAKE HANDLE

FOLD

CARDBOARD

GLUE ON SPONGE OR STRING DESIGN

FOLD

SCRAPE AWAY EXCESS

SOAP

DRAW DESIGN

CUT AWAY OR CARVE OUT THE DESIGN

ERASER

Or, glue string onto the base instead of sponges.

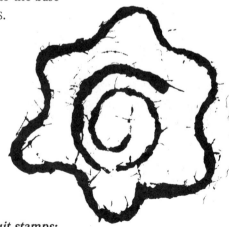

Vegetable and fruit stamps: See pages 61–62.

Sticker Madness

Stickers, stickers, stickers! You see them everywhere! Go for a really fancy sparkle look, pick your favorite animals or sports, make sticker borders, choose an alphabet font that suits your scrapbooking style, or design a whole page.

BORDER STICKERS

FLOWER STICKER BORDER

ALPHABET STICKERS

STICKER COVER DESIGN

STICKER DESIGNS ON INSIDE PAGES

Sticker Savvy

Here are some tips for some not-so-ordinary sticker designs:

POP-UP

STICKER WITH BACKING

3-D effect. Trim around the sticker, leaving the back covering on. Place pop-ups (page 11) on the back of the sticker and place it on your page. Awesome!

Action moves. Overlap three or four stickers of the same design.

Far-out frames. Cut out stickers, leaving the backs on. Using a pencil, lightly draw a frame outline. Place the stickers down with their backs still on until you're happy with the design, then remove the backings and stick them in place.

Tricks of the Trade

Practice first. Leave the backs on your stickers and move them around your page to find where you like them best. Then remove the backing and stick them on.

Stick and hold. Cut stickers in half for corner designs or use them to hold a photo or artwork in place.

STICKERS HOLDING MAT

Slick sticker storage. Use plastic sleeves made for trading cards to hold your stickers. That way, you can see what you have, know where they are, and keep them organized.

Easy Custom-Designed Stickers

Store-bought stickers are cool, but sometimes your own design works best!

Materials

❧ Old magazines
❧ Scissors
❧ Homemade Stickum

   1 tablespoon (15 ml)
      flavored gelatin mix*

   2 tablespoons (30 ml)
      boiling water

❧ Heatproof container
❧ Paintbrush

If you don't have flavored gelatin, use 1 packet ($^1/_4$ oz/6.25 g) unflavored gelatin mixed with 1 tablespoon (15 ml) sugar and $^1/_4$ cup (50 ml) boiling water. Add a few drops of flavoring (like vanilla) if desired.

Let's do it!

1. Cut out artwork, paper shapes, or pictures from magazines.

2. With an adult helper, mix the gelatin and boiling water together in the container until the gelatin dissolves.

3. Brush the gelatin mixture on the backs of the cutouts. Let dry. When you're ready to use the sticker, just lick it and stick it in place.

Store leftover Homemade Stickum in a covered container in the fridge. If it sets to a hard gelatin, just place the container in a pan of hot water. It will turn back into a liquid!

Photography Fun

Lights, camera, action! One of the most interesting parts of any scrapbook is the photos. And for photo albums, well, photos are the main attraction! You probably already have a few stacks of photos just waiting to be put into place. Here's all you need to know to make the very best display in your albums!

Cropping & Composition

The more you use your camera, the better your pictures will be. But your prints don't have to be perfect to go into your album. If you like just part of a picture, you can *crop* (trim away) the parts that you don't want, to improve the overall look. Cropping also helps make room on your page for more photos. Sometimes cropping just means cutting off the end of a photo; other times you may want to cut out a shape, or even the entire subject!

SIMPLE CROPPING

CUT AWAY THE EDGES

CUT LINE

CUT LINE

CUT LINES

CUT LINE

CUT LINE

CUT OUT SUBJECT

Crop Like a Pro!

Decide what shape and size your photo should be *before* you cut it by using homemade L-shaped cropping frames. All you need is a pencil, ruler, tracing paper, scissors, cardboard, and some tape.

To make the cardboard L's:
Trace the PHOTO CROPPING template on page 119 onto tracing paper. Using that pattern, trace the shape twice onto cereal-box cardboard. Cut out the cardboard "croppers" and strengthen the edges with masking tape.

To crop the photo:

1. Fold tracing paper around the print you'd like to crop. Tape it to the back of the print with masking tape.

2. Move the croppers around, sliding them up and down and from side to side — even tilted — until you have the look you like. Lightly mark the cropped shape onto the tracing paper.

CUT OUT CROPPED AREA

3. Remove the tracing paper and cut along the lines. Place it back on the photo. If you like what you see, you can cut the photo to size or enlarge or reduce it on a color copier or photocopier.

Note: Polaroid photos should not be cut — the chemicals used in processing can leak out and damage your pages.

CROPPED-AND-CUT PHOTO

CARDBOARD L'S

MASKING TAPE

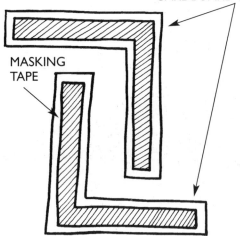

MARKED CROPPING LINES

TRACING PAPER

Tricks of the Trade

Photo shapes. Use cutout stencils (page 90) as photo mounts, or design your own! Make a PHOTO FLOWER (page 95), or fill in a frame of butterfly wings, pumpkins, beach balls, beach umbrellas, or soccer balls!

Photo Flower

Trace the PHOTO FLOWER template (page 120) onto tracing paper and cut it out. Use this tracing-paper pattern to cut the flower shape out of card stock. Then arrange the photos, starting with the center. When you like the effect, cut out the photos, glue in place onto the card stock, and outline the flower with a permanent marker.

1. TRACE THE CIRCLE AND PETALS

2. ARRANGE PHOTOS; TRACE AND CUT TO FIT FLOWER SHAPES

3. GLUE CIRCLE PHOTO

4. GLUE PETAL PHOTOS

5. OUTLINE WITH MARKER

Compose It!

How you arrange your photos together on your page is called the *composition.*

To start, look through your photos and decide which you think would look good or fit well together on a page. Look for color combinations, subjects, or activities that relate to one another. Move your photos around to test them out. Do they all fit? Should some of them be cropped, or do you want all your photographs the same size? Maybe photo cutouts best fit your design. Consider what else you'll be adding to your page, too.

Large and small. Choose one large picture for the center and add smaller pictures around it. You can even enlarge a photo to make a background.

PHOTO CUTOUT

DECORATIVE PAPER BORDER

ENLARGED BACKGROUND PHOTO

Overlaps. Don't be afraid to overlap your pictures for a "collage" look!

Try a mat. Sometimes making a border or mat around the photo gives it a little more interest and "breathing room." It can also help add color or tie a page together. (For more about making mats and edged designs, see page 78).

OVERLAPPED PHOTOS

CORRUGATED CARDBOARD BACKGROUND

STRIPED MAT

PHOTO CUTOUTS

MAT WITH EDGED DESIGN

Making the Mount Count

How you decide to mount your photos will impact your display, too.

Photo sleeves, those clear plastic pages with slots to slip photos in and out, are easy to use. Most are so uniform, however, that they don't offer a lot of creativity to the design of the page.

Mounting corners allow you to position photos (or other items) anywhere on the page. And it's simple to lift the pictures in and out. You can buy them, or — better yet — make your own!

SIMPLE NO-FOLD CORNERS

STORE-BOUGHT CORNERS: JUST LICK AND STICK!

SIMPLE NO-FOLD CORNERS

CUT PAPER TRIANGLES; GLUE TO ALBUM PAGE

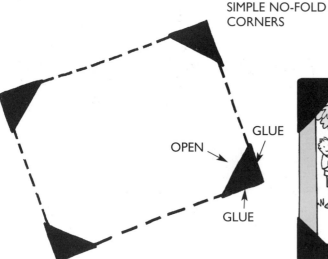

OPEN

GLUE

GLUE

october 10th 2000

Cheetahs Rule!

Baily Park • Long Beach

HANDMADE FOLDED MOUNTING CORNERS

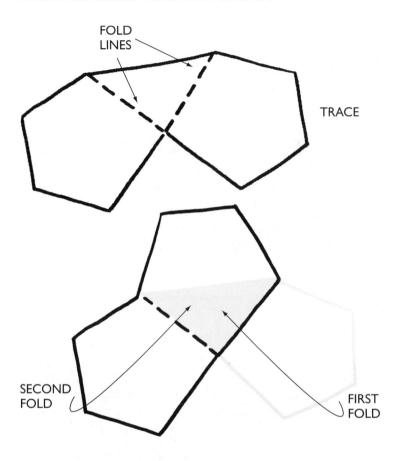

FOLD
LINES

TRACE

SECOND
FOLD

SECOND
FOLD

FIRST
FOLD

FRONT VIEW

INSERT
PHOTO

Pop-ups give a terrific 3-D effect! Glue photos to card stock for support, then cut out the subjects and attach pop-up stickers (page 11) to the photo back and page.

Tricks of the Trade

Use a pocket. The best photo albums have a place for everything, including extra photos and negatives. You can buy all sorts of plastic pockets. To make your own, tape rectangles of paper about 4" x 8" (10 x 20 cm) to your pages. Or make the fancier version on page 17.

Special Effects

Try these for some extra photography fun!

Photo Mix-up

Tickle your funny bone with a totally mixed-up photo page. Draw body art, cut graphics from cards or other printed materials, or mix up different photographs to make a silly display!

CUT OUT HEADS FROM PHOTOS

STICKERS OR FUNNY CARDS

Make a Scene

One of my favorite album techniques is to cut out pictures and place them in a background scene. You can copy pictures from a book and put your photos in the scene, use old cards as a backdrop for photos, or make an artwork background. Make it as realistic or as silly as you want.

GLUE CUTOUT
PHOTOS TO CARDS

GLUE CUTOUT PHOTOS TO CARDS

COPY PICTURES FROM
BOOKS OR MAGAZINES;
GLUE CUTOUT PHOTOS

An Old-Fashioned Silhouette

An outline, or *silhouette*, of a person (or favorite pet) can give the effect of a photograph but add a whole new look to your album. Try silhouetting different people, action shots, your pet, or even your favorite cartoon character!

Materials

> *General supplies:* tracing paper, pencil, scissors, glue
> Photo (a profile shot works best)
> Black or colored construction paper
> Background paper

Let's do it!

1. Make a photocopy of the picture to use (so you won't ruin the original). Enlarge it if you like.

2. Place the tracing paper on top of the picture; gently trace around the profile.

3. Place the traced picture on top of the black or colored paper. Holding both pieces together, cut out the shape.

4. Mount the construction-paper silhouette on a solid or printed background.

Tricks of the Trade

Make a shadow. Add the silhouette to the original picture to get a 3-D effect.

Light on black ... Make several silhouettes to use as die cuts and message balloons (page 114). Use gel pens to write your message!

... and black on white. Take a roll of black-and-white pictures for a very different look!

Creative Lettering & Journaling

Placing your awesome photos and other special stuff in your albums is just one part of what scrapbooking is all about: There's also all the details, like captions, titles, and cool lettering to set your pages off! This is where your personal style really shines through. Your *journaling* (what you write in your album) can be as simple or as detailed as you want it to be. The important thing is that it comes from you. Make it as creative (and as fun) as you are!

Take-a-Look Lettering

Take a look around you at all the signs, advertisements, and printed words you see. What color combos and letter styles catch your eye? Lettering plays a big part in attracting your attention! Cool lettering (done by you!) can do the same thing for your scrapbook or photo album. Experiment with different styles. You can buy page toppers, stickers, tracing stencils, and stamps in all sorts of lettering designs. Or, make up your own letter combos from old cards or magazines, computer fonts, or even string!

LETTER COLLAGE

ALPHABET STICKERS

STORE-BOUGHT PAGE TOPPERS

TRACED LETTERS FROM STENCILS

MATTED PEN ART

Now

Wonderful!

STAMPS

STAMPED LETTERS

ADVENTURE

COOL COMPUTER FONTS

LAURA

LAURA

Laura

LAURA

Say It in String!

Looking for something special? Try writing a word or name in string. Cut the string to the length you'll need (you'll have to practice writing in string to find just the right amount), then write the word in glue and place the string on top.

PLACE STRING IN GLUE "WRITING"

Pens, Pens & More Pens!

The most original lettering, of course, is your very own handwriting. There are all sorts of ways to add pizzazz to your handwriting, using different pens and lettering styles. The more doodles, the better!

Before you ink the page, practice writing the same word with several different-styled pens and colors. You might want a fine-point pen for outlining and wider tips for filling in detail art or making broad strokes. Some pens are easier to work with than others. (Calligraphy pens, for instance, take a bit of practice.) Scroll tips are nice for borders, and opaque or *gel-ink pens* (the type with ink that comes out like paint and takes a few minutes to dry) show up really well on colored papers.

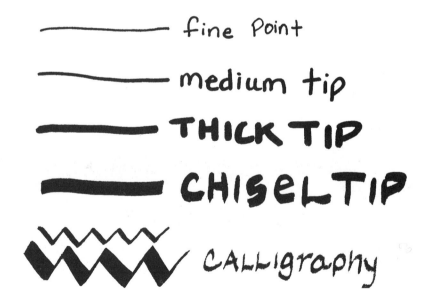

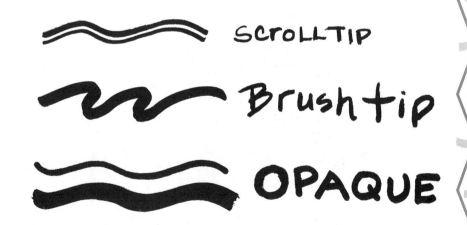

Tricks of the Trade

Inks & Other Ideas

- For really long-lasting results, use pigment ink and waterproof, fade-resistant pens. You can buy special memory-book pens in various colors.

- Practice on scrap paper. Try keeping your letters straight up and down and evenly spaced, using a faint ruler line (you can erase it later). Try capitals and lowercase letters, and different styles, such as TALL AND THIN letters or SHORT AND WIDE printing.

AaBbCcDd **AaBbCcDd**

TALL AND THIN or SHORT AND WIDE
TALL AND THIN   SHORT AND WIDE

- Please pass the jelly? Gel-ink pens roll out smooth, bright colors. They even come in metallic and glitter inks. "Jellies" make writing and doodling an adventure!

- Try crayons!

Make a Quill Pen!

Try some old-time writing, using a colonial-style quill pen that you make yourself! The colonists used goose, turkey, crow, or hawk feathers, but you can use a feather from a craft store. This creates unusual writing — just don't expect it to be as fast and easy as a modern-day ballpoint!

Materials

- 8" to 12" (20 to 30 cm) feather
- Warm, soapy water
- Scissors
- Sharp knife (for adult use only)
- Cutting board
- Ink (store-bought or homemade)
- Paper towels

QUILL

Let's do it!

1. Soak the feather in the water until it softens (about 15 minutes). Pluck or use scissors to strip the bottom feathers away from the *quill* (the hollow shaft of the feather), leaving 2" (5 cm) of bare quill.

2. Have an adult cut the end of the feather at a slight angle to make the *nib*, or writing point, and then cut a *small* slit at the end to control the flow of the ink.

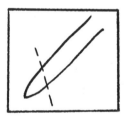

1. CUT AT ANGLE

2. CUT A SLIT

3. Dip the quill into ink and gently blot the tip on a paper towel to remove the excess.

4. Practice writing on paper, holding the quill at different angles. Re-dip and blot the quill as needed (you'll have to do this step a lot!). Experiment until you get a line you like. If the nib wears down, repeat step 2 to cut a new one.

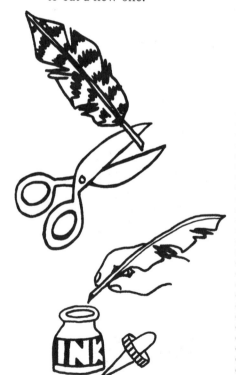

Very Berry Ink

Make your own ink from ripe blackberries, strawberries, or raspberries! Use a spoon and strainer to crush about a cup (250 ml) of berries (crush a few at a time, then refill the strainer). Let the juice drip into a jar — that's the part you want. Once all the berries have been squeezed into juice, add a teaspoon (5 ml) each of vinegar and salt. Stir until the salt dissolves. Use your ink immediately. To make it darker, add a drop of red or blue food coloring.

Extra-Special Lettering

Now that you've gotten comfortable with your pens, try some special lettering techniques. Then combine techniques to create your own awesome effect!

Separate letters with dots, stars, hearts, or other doodles.

Outline bold letters with a fine tip in a different shade.

F·e·b·r·u·a·r·y

S·T·A·R·S

J·U·L·Y

H·E·A·R·T·S

c·i·r·c·l·e·s

S·W·I·R·L·S

AWESOME

SUPER! COOL!

OUTLINE THEM

Tricks of the Trade

Oops? Remember, there are no "mistakes" — any lettering surprises are simply a new twist on the design! For off-center words or letters that go haywire, add a sticker or turn the mark into doodle art! If you really want to redo a letter, ink out the original with a correction pen, available from office supply stores.

Write on a curve

Write on a **curve**.

stagger letters

Stagger letters.

TRY SOME DOTS

Add dots where lines connect.

Try some **delicate swirls**.

Add Swirls

jazz it up

Add **details** to jazz it up!

Make **bold letters** for titles and page toppers, and fill in the letters with designs and patterns.

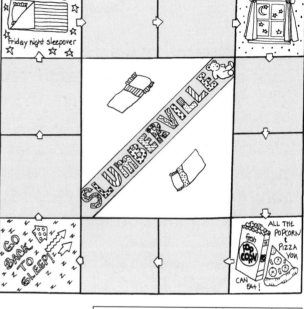

Print each letter separately, then cut out and glue onto the page.

Combine techniques.

Just-Right Journaling

Part of the fun of a scrapbook is looking back months or even years from now at what you did. Even though the events are fresh in your mind right now, it's amazing how fast details and names can fade from our memories! Also, photos and mementos don't tell the whole story. You might also want to tell about funny things that happened.

That's where the journaling comes in. It's simply adding the five W's — the *who, what, when, where*, and *why* — to your pages. With something you collected, you might want to tell when you got it, why it is so special, who you were with, and where you were. You can write a little or a lot; whatever you feel like writing is fine. For photos, you might tell the date, who is in the picture, and what you were doing — as well as who took the photo and isn't shown! Add your messages in a funny design or in matted boxes, or use fancy lettering (pages 109–110). Remember, there are no rules except what you decide using your imagination!

Write On!

When writing captions, the words don't always have to go under a photo or object. You can add them anywhere!

Don't feel like writing while you're busy laying out a page?

That's fine! Lots of scrapbookers lay out the pages first and then come back later to add the captions or notes. My favorite technique (so I won't forget to leave space for my writing) is to make a mat box and leave it blank so I can write in it later.

Or, make die cuts or message balloons for later entries (see page 114) — you can even buy journaling stamps that have blank lines! Another option is to simply leave some white space on your page to fill in later. The trick is to plan ahead, so you save space for info you want to add.

BLANK BOX FOR WRITING IN LATER

JOURNALING BOX WITH LINES

BLANK BOX FOR WRITING IN LATER

Make a word frame. Write your message around the entire page, or around and around an individual photo or memento.

Rhyme time. Say what you mean with a made-up poem or lyrics from a favorite song. You can even write your rhyme in a word frame!

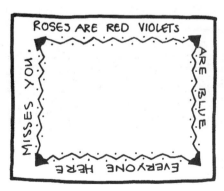

Photo message. Make your message part of a photo, or use a photo as a background. Write the name of where you were in the sand at the beach or by a river. Include photos of trail signs, streets, or other signs.

TRAIL SIGN

TREE TRUNK PHOTO AS BACKGROUND FOR CAPTION

FUN INFO

Die cuts and message balloons.
Write your message inside a die cut, or around and around on the inside. Or, use the cartoonist's trick and make a message balloon! (For templates, see page 122.)

Rebus art. Create a picture sentence mixing words with pictures and stickers.

YOU ARE A STAR

HAPPY THOUGHTS!

Flap cards. Make a small card, pull up the flap, and write your message inside!

YOUR STAR SHINES BRIGHT!

MY HEART IS YOURS NOW AND FOREVER. YOU ARE THE ONE.

Tricks of the Trade

Make the news! Recording a really special day or event in your life? Cut out the headlines from the newspapers that day to include what was happening around the world at the same time.

Tell all. Add what's happening that's *not* in the picture — the smells, sounds, other people who where there, etc. If you enjoy writing and keeping diaries, write a short paragraph that includes everything you can remember. Later, you'll be able to relive the adventure!

Templates

Gift Envelope

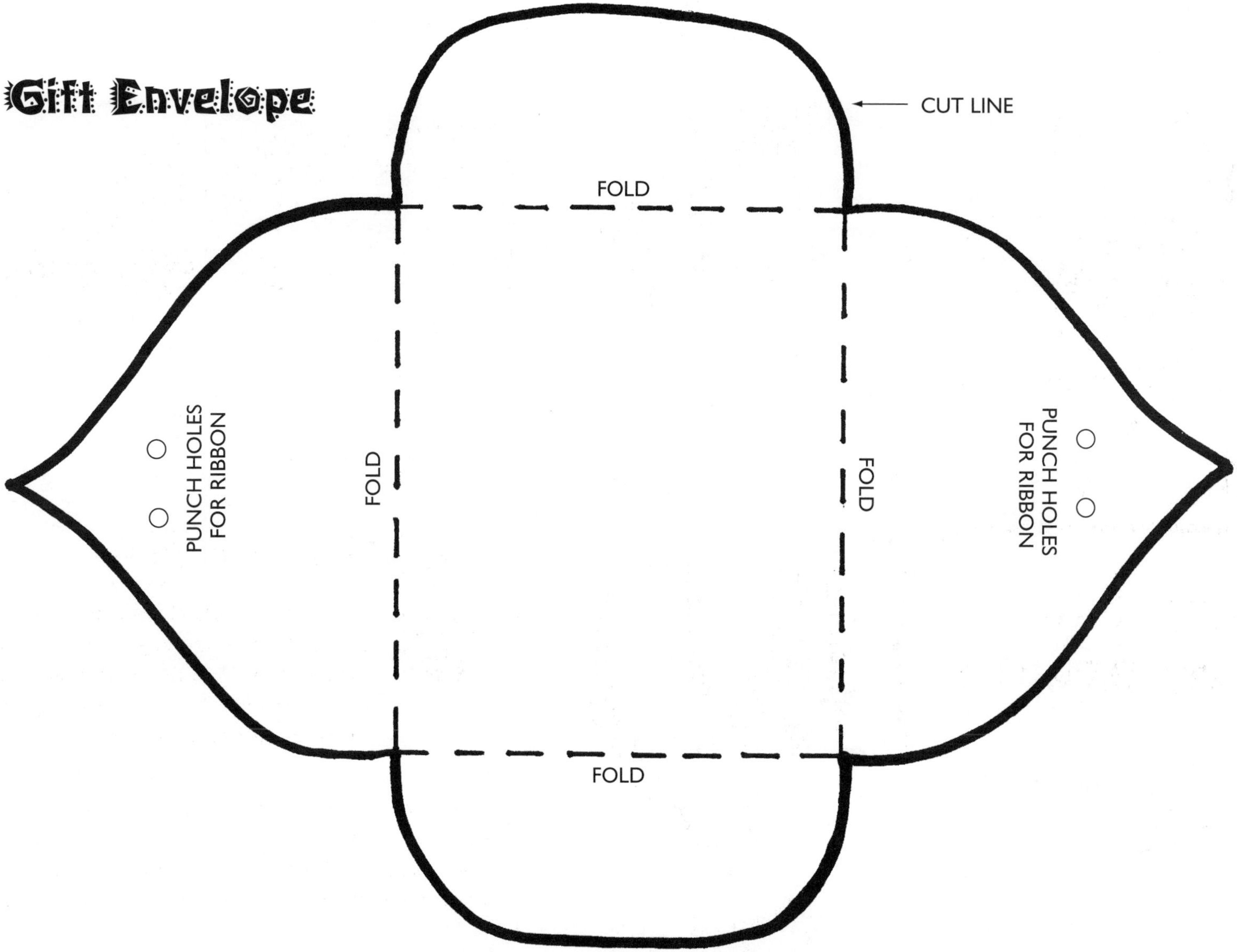

CUT LINE

FOLD

FOLD

FOLD

FOLD

PUNCH HOLES
FOR RIBBON

PUNCH HOLES
FOR RIBBON

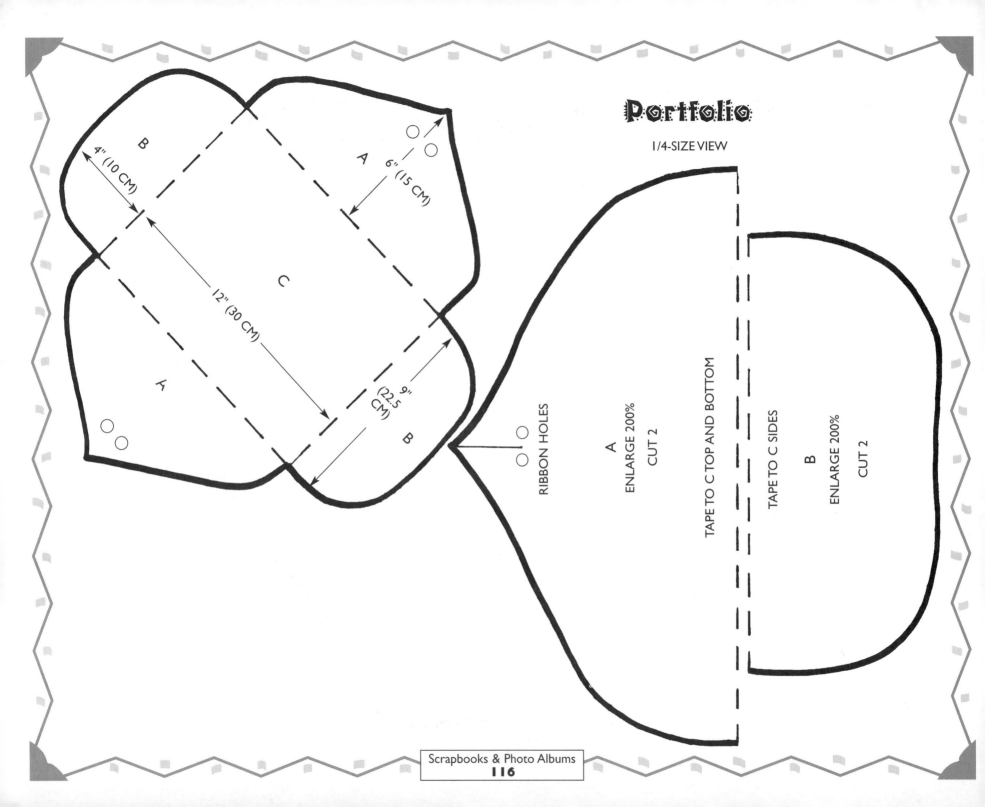

Portfolio

1/4-SIZE VIEW

B

A

6" (15 CM)

4" (10 CM)

C

12" (30 CM)

A

9" (22.5 CM)

B

RIBBON HOLES

A
ENLARGE 200%
CUT 2

TAPE TO C TOP AND BOTTOM

TAPE TO C SIDES

B
ENLARGE 200%
CUT 2

Apple Pocket

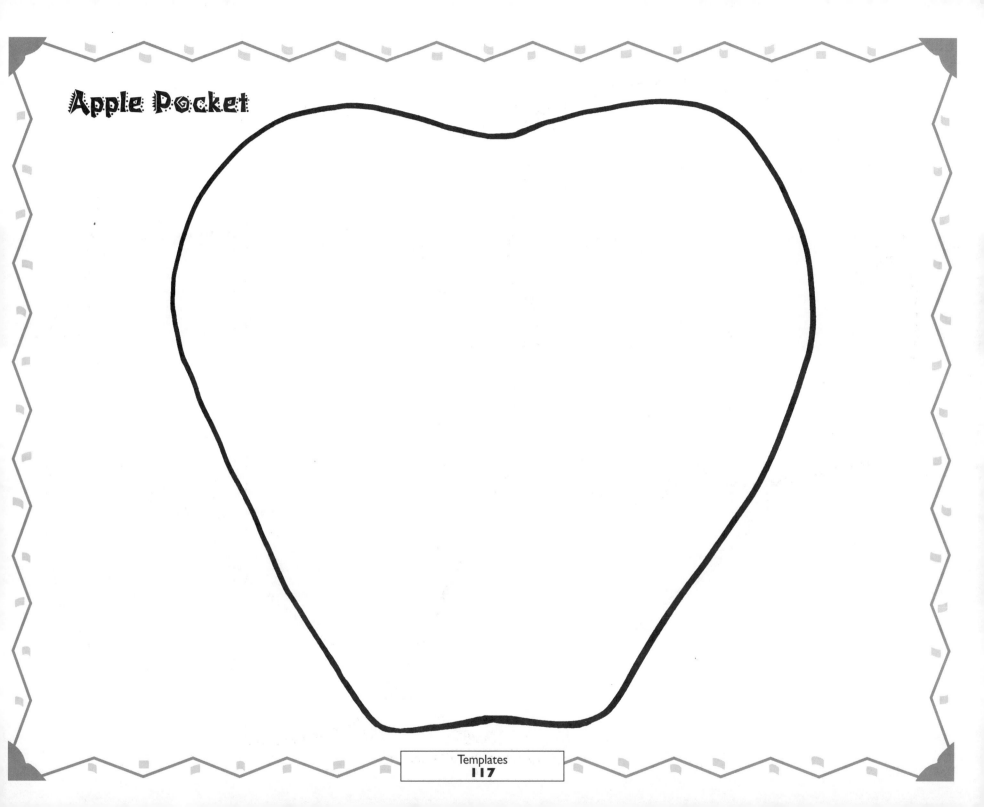

Heart Pocket

Photo Cropping

TRACE AND CUT LINE

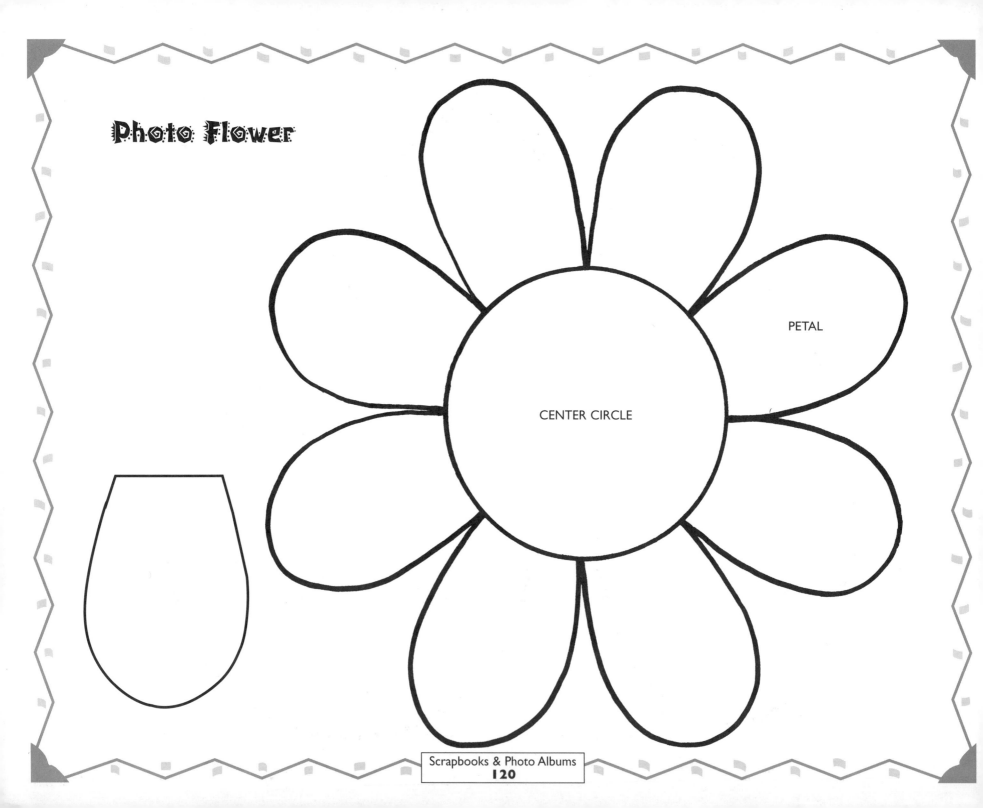

Photo Flower

PETAL

CENTER CIRCLE

Photo & Caption

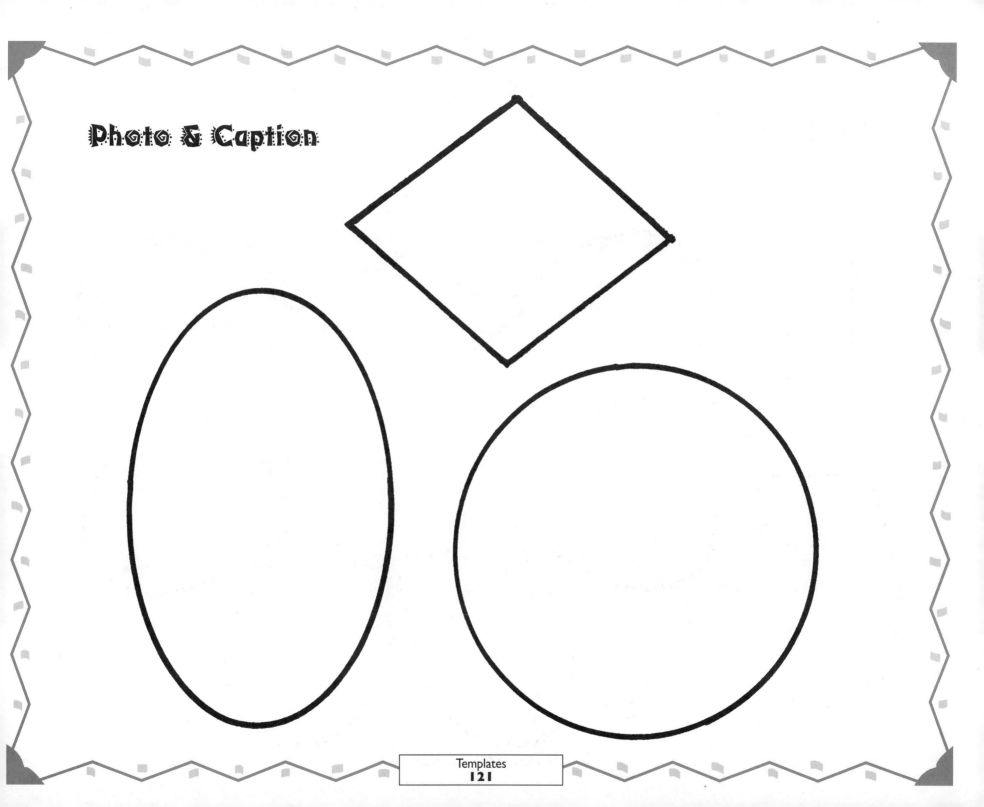

Photo & Caption

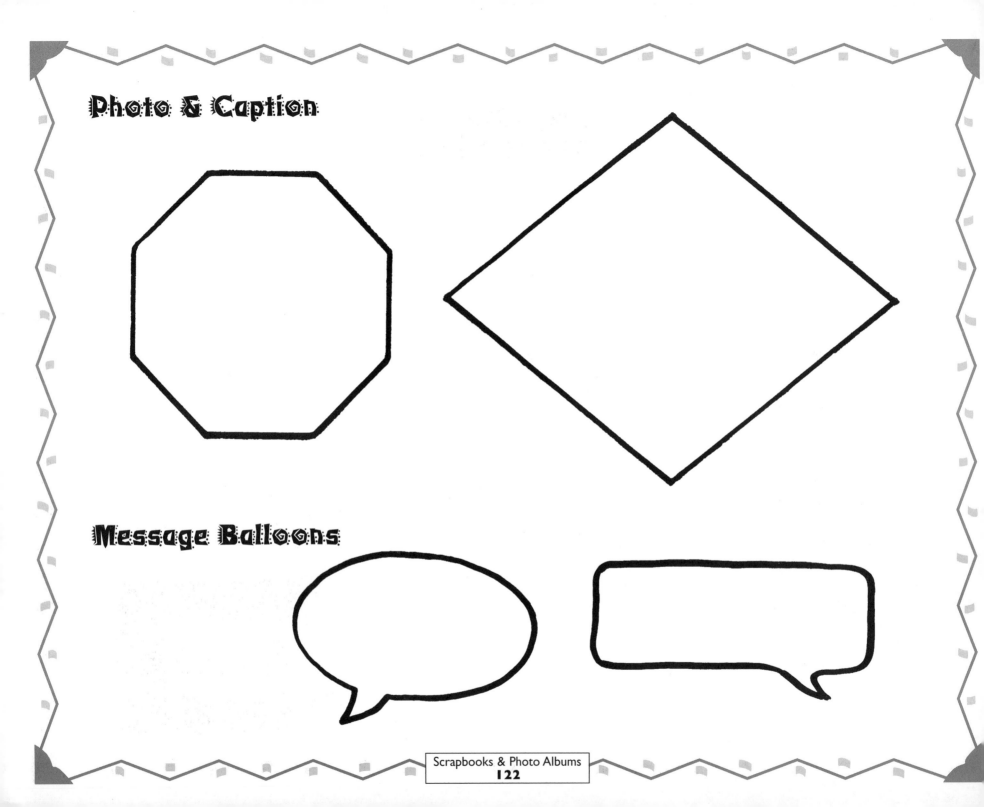

Message Balloons

Index

A

accordion album, 32–33
adhesives. *See* glue and adhesives
albums, 24–38
    Awesome Accordion Album, 32–33
    Buddy Books, 30–31
    Easy Loose-Ring Binder, 26–27
    Hole-Punch Design, 28–29
    magnetic, 9
    Photo or Art Folder, 25
    post-bound albums, 36–37, 50–51
    spiral-bound albums, 38
    Wrap-Around Album, 34–35
    See also covers
archival (acid-free) materials, 9, 53
art
    Art Folder, 25
    chalk rubbings, 70
    handmade paper, 73–75
    rebus art, 114
    tissue-paper art, 66
    See also painting and printing

B

backgrounds, 101. *See also* papers
binders, 9, 29, 50–51
    Easy Loose-Ring Binder, 26–27
    three-ring binder covers, 42–51
borders, 8, 80, 82, 84, 89, 106. *See also* rulers;
    scissors
Buddy Books, 30–31

C

calligraphy, 106
captions, 111–114, 121–122
chalk rubbings, 70
collecting, 21
    bulky items, 7, 9, 16, 26
    materials and tools, 7, 9
containers. *See* file boxes; pockets; sleeves,
    plastic; trays, 3-D
cookie cutters, 9, 84
corners
    cutting corners, 10
    mounting corners, 11, 98–99
covers, 39–51
    Decorated Canvas Cover, 50–51
    decoupage theme covers, 40–41
    Denim Cover, 44–45
    Felt Design Cover, 42–43
    Padded Fabric Cover, 46–49
    poster board covers, 8
    See also albums
cropping, 93–95, 118

D

decoupage, 40–41
die cuts, 7, 8, 82–83, 114

E

edgers, 7, 77–78
embellishments, 76–91. *See also* die cuts;
    lettering; punches; scissors; stamps;
    stickers
eraser stamp, 88

F

fabric
    Decorated Canvas Cover, 50–51
    Denim Cover, 44–45
    Felt Design Cover, 42–43
    Padded Fabric Cover, 46–49
    right vs. wrong side, 45
    yarn stitching, 45
file boxes, 23
finger paint, 68
flap cards, 114
folders, 25
frames, 48–49, 82, 90, 113. *See also* mats
friendship books, 30–31

G

gift envelopes, 18, 31, 115
glues and adhesives, 10–11
    for decoupage, 41
    for felt covers, 42
    homemade stickum recipe, 91
    mounting corners, 11, 98–99
    pop-ups, 11, 99

H

Hole-Punch Design Album, 28–29

I

ink, 87, 107, 108. *See also* pens

J

journaling, 103, 111–114

L

lace-up album, 28–29
laminating, 14–15
layout. *See* borders; captions; frames; mats;
    photographs
lettering, 103–110
    pens, 106–108
    string letters, 105
    styles and fonts, 104–105
    techniques, 109–110

M

magnetic albums, 9
marbleized paper, 71–72
materials, 7, 9, 28–29
    archival materials, 9, 53
    storage, 15

See also die cuts; papers; pockets; sleeves,
    plastic; stickers
mats, 97
    making, 8, 12–13, 81, 85
    stickers and, 90
    See also frames
memorabilia, sorting, 21–23
message balloons, 8, 114, 122
mounting corners, 11, 98–99

N

natural materials, 9, 26–27, 61–62, 63

P

painting and printing
    finger paint recipe, 68
    finger prints, 64
    found-object prints, 60
    marbleized paper, 71–72
    nature prints, 63
    paper prints, 66
    potato and vegetable prints, 61–62
    sole prints, 65
    splatter-paint designs, 58
    sponge-stamped designs, 55–57
    string-dipped designs, 59
    watercolor paintings, 69
papers, 7, 9, 52–75
    archival (acid-free) papers, 9, 53
    handmade paper, 73–75
    homemade decorative papers, 54–72
    tea-aged paper, 75
    types, 8, 53
    See also painting and printing
pencil, photo-marking, 22
pens, 7, 8, 106, 107
    glue pens, 10
    photographs and, 22

quill pens, 108
photographs, 93–102
    attaching, 10, 11, 90, 98–99
    background scenes, 101
    captions, 111–114
    composition and layout, 96–97
    cookie-cutter photo mats, 85
    cropping, 93–95, 118
    Padded Photo Frame, 48–49
    Photo Flower, 95, 120
    Photo Folder, 25
    photo messages, 113
    photo mix-up, 100
    recording information on, 22
    silhouettes, 102
    storage, 23
    templates, 120–122
    See also frames; mats
pockets, 7, 16–19
    apple pocket template, 117
    attaching paper pockets, 10
    felt pocket, 43
    folders, 25
    heart pocket template, 117
    laminated objects, 14
    making pockets, 16–18, 99
    storing extras in, 19
    See also sleeves, plastic; zip-locking bags
pop-ups, 11, 99
portfolio template, 116
post-bound albums, 36–37, 50–51
poster board, 8
potato prints, 61–62
punches, 7, 79–81

Q

quill pens, 108

R

recipes
  berry ink, 108
  finger paint, 68
  homemade stickum, 91
reinforcement circles, 9, 31
rings, 9, 26, 27. *See also* binders
rulers, 7

S

safety, 15
scissors, 7, 41, 77–78
shoe prints, 65
silhouettes, 57–58, 102
sleeves, plastic, 7, 9, 16, 98. *See also* pockets;
  zip-locking bags
soap stamp, 88
sorting memorabilia, 21–23
spiral-bound albums, 38
sponge stamp, 55–57, 88
stamps, 86–88
  rubber stamps, 7, 86–87
  vegetable/food stamps, 61–62
stencils, 7, 81, 84–85, 94, 104. *See also*
  templates
stickers, 7, 89–91
storage, 7, 23, 87. *See also* pockets; sleeves,
  plastic
string, 59, 105
supplies. *See* materials; tools

T

techniques and tips, 10–19
  cutting at an angle, 41
  cutting corners, 10
  decoupage, 41
  design arrangement, 41
  edgers, 77–78
  glues and adhesives, 10–11, 42
  journaling and captions, 114
  laces, designer, 31
  laminating, 14–15
  lettering, 106–107, 109
  marbleized paper, 71–72
  mats, 12–13
  painting/printing techniques, 55–66, 68–69
  papermaking, 73–75
  patterns for borders and backgrounds, 63
  photo cropping, 93–95
  rubber stamping, 87
  safety, 15
  silhouettes, 102
  sponge cutting, 56
  stencils, 84
  sticker designs, 90
  tea-aged paper, 75
  yarn-stitched covers, 45
  zip-locking bags, 26
  See also specific projects
templates, 7
  apple pocket, 117
  cropping templates, 10, 94, 119
  gift envelope, 115
  heart pocket, 118
  message balloons, 122
  Photo Flower, 120
  photo/caption, 121–122
  portfolio, 116
  See also stencils

tissue-paper art, 66
tools, 7, 9
  photo-marking pencil, 22
  punches, 7, 79–81
  safety and storage, 15
  scissors, 7, 41, 77–78
  See also pens; stamps; stencils; templates
trays, 3-D, 7, 16

V

vegetable prints, 61–62

W

watercolors, 69
Wrap-Around Album, 34–35

Z

zip-locking bags, 26–27. *See also* sleeves, plastic

More Good Books from Williamson Publishing

Williamson books are available from your bookseller or directly from Williamson Publishing. Please see last page for ordering information or to visit our website. Thank you.

Williamson's *Kids Can!*® **books ...**

Kids Can!® books are 128 to 176 pages, fully illustrated, trade paper, 11 x 8½, $12.95 US/ $19.95 CAN.

American Bookseller Pick of the Lists
Dr. Toy Best Vacation Product
KIDS' CRAZY ART CONCOCTIONS
50 Mysterious Mixtures for Art & Craft Fun
by Jill Frankel Hauser

Parents' Choice Recommended
KIDS' ART WORKS!
Creating with Color, Design, Texture & More
by Sandi Henry

Teachers' Choice Award
Parent's Guide Children's Media Award
Dr. Toy Best Vacation Product
CUT-PAPER PLAY!
Dazzling Creations from Construction Paper
by Sandi Henry

Parents' Choice Approved
Parent's Guide Children's Media Award
MAKING COOL CRAFTS & AWESOME ART!
A Kids' Treasure Trove of Fabulous Fun
by Roberta Gould

Parents' Choice Gold Award
American Bookseller Pick of the Lists
Oppenheim Toy Portfolio Gold Award
THE KIDS' MULTICULTURAL ART BOOK
Art & Craft Experiences from Around the World
by Alexandra M. Terzian

JAZZY JEWELRY
Power Beads, Crystals, Chokers, & Illusion and Tattoo Styles
by Diane Baker

American Bookseller Pick of the Lists
Parents' Choice Recommended
ADVENTURES IN ART
Arts & Crafts Experiences for 8- to 13-Year-Olds
by Susan Milord

Benjamin Franklin Best Education/ Teaching Gold Award
Parent's Guide Children's Media Award
HAND-PRINT ANIMAL ART
by Carolyn Carreiro
full color, $12.95

American Bookseller Pick of the Lists
Parents' Choice Approved
Oppenheim Toy Portfolio Gold Award
SUMMER FUN!
60 Activities for a Kid-Perfect Summer
by Susan Williamson

Williamson's

Quick Starts for Kids!™ books ...

The following *Quick Starts for Kids!*™ books for children, ages 8 and older, are each 64 pages, fully illustrated, trade paper, 8 x 10, $7.95 US/ $10.95 CAN.

GARDEN FUN!
Grow a Pizza, a Rainbow ... & More!
by Vicky Congdon

40 KNOTS TO KNOW!
Hitches, Loops, Bends & Bindings
by Emily Stetson

MAKE YOUR OWN FUN PICTURE FRAMES!
by Matt Phillips

MAKE YOUR OWN HAIRWEAR!
Beaded Barrettes, Clips, Dangles & Headbands
by Diane Baker

Parents' Choice Recommended
BAKE THE BEST-EVER COOKIES!
by Sarah A. Williamson

BE A CLOWN!
Techniques from a Real Clown
by Ron Burgess

WITHDRAWN

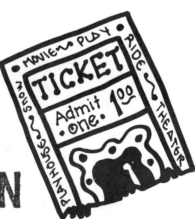

Dr. Toy 100 Best Children's Products
Dr. Toy 10 Best Socially Responsible Products
MAKE YOUR OWN BIRDHOUSES & FEEDERS
by Robyn Haus

YO-YO!
Tips & Tricks from a Real Pro
by Ron Burgess

Oppenheim Toy Portfolio Gold Award
DRAW YOUR OWN CARTOONS!
by Don Mayne

KIDS' EASY KNITTING PROJECTS
by Peg Blanchette

KIDS' EASY QUILTING PROJECTS
by Terri Thibault

American Booksellers Pick of the Lists
MAKE YOUR OWN TEDDY BEARS & BEAR CLOTHES
by Sue Mahren

Visit Our Website!

To see what's new at Williamson and learn more about specific books, visit our website at:

www.williamsonbooks.com

To Order Books:

You'll find Williamson books wherever high-quality children's books are sold, or order directly from Williamson Publishing. We accept Visa and MasterCard *(please include the number and expiration date)*.

Toll-free phone orders with credit cards:
1-800-234-8791

Or, send a check with your order to:
**Williamson Publishing Company
P.O. Box 185
Charlotte, Vermont 05445**

Catalog request: **mail, phone, or e-mail <info@williamsonbooks.com>**

Please add **$4.00** for postage for one book plus **$1.00** for each additional book. Satisfaction is guaranteed or full refund without questions or quibbles.